To Mac.
Merry
From. M

VICTORIAN AND EDWARDIAN
ANGUS
FROM RARE PHOTOGRAPHS

VICTORIAN AND EDWARDIAN
ANGUS
FROM RARE PHOTOGRAPHS

RAYMOND LAMONT-BROWN
AND
PETER ADAMSON

FOREWORD
BY
The Rt Hon The Earl of Airlie, KT, GCVO, DL

ALVIE PUBLICATIONS ST ANDREWS

First published 1986 by
Alvie Publications
52 Buchanan Gardens
St Andrews KY16 9LX
(Tel: 0334 75227)

ISBN 0 9511800 0 2

Printed in Scotland by
Spectrum Printing Company Limited
Livingston

Contents

ACKNOWLEDGEMENTS

The compilers of this volume would like to express their gratitude and thanks to Peter Brockes, Reference Librarian, BP Library of Motoring, Beaulieu; Mrs Elizabeth M Drainer, National Trust For Scotland, Representative at Barrie's Birthplace and the Angus Folk Museum, at Kirriemuir and Glamis respectively; C P Atkins, Librarian ,National Railway Museum, York; Michael Mutch, Motor Museum, Aberlady; The Hon James Ogilvy; Mr Bill Harvey, Dept of Civil Engineering, University of Dundee; Ms Margaret King, Signal Tower Museum, Arbroath; David Adams; Mr & Mrs R Robertson, The Retreat; G N Drummond, Director of Libraries and Museums, Angus District Council; W Graham Watson, Assistant Curator, Montrose Museum; J B Russell, Broughty Ferry; Ms Elsie Greig, Forfar; Mr J MacRitchie, Kirriemuir Library; Miss Margaret Bruce, Kirriemuir; Martin Baxter, General Manager, Swallow Hotel, Invergowrie; George Smith, Forfar; Mrs Enid Gauldie, Invergowrie; J B Ramage, Chief Librarian, City of Dundee District Council; Rev Charles W Miller, Liff; Mrs Joan Auld, Archivist, The Library, University of Dundee; R Nimmo, Rector, High School of Dundee; Mrs Mary Carstairs, Kirriemuir . . . for their unfailing advice, help and encouragement in the collection of the rare photographs herein, without which the book would not have been possible.

Raymond Lamont-Brown would particularly like to thank Her Majesty Queen Elizabeth the Queen Mother for graciously commenting on the photographs from the collection at Glamis Castle and to her Private Secretary and Equerry Lt Col Sir Martin Gilliat for his courtesy in assisting in this matter. Raymond Lamont-Brown offers a special thanks too to his friends the Earl and Countess of Strathmore and Kinghorne for their kind help with the Glamis pictures and to the Castle Administrator Col T D Lloyd-Jones. Grateful thanks too go to George Shepherd, editor of the Arbroath Herald, and Mrs Elizabeth Drainer, Kirriemuir, for the kind assistance given in compiling the captions relating to their subjects.

The authors especially wish to thank The Rt Hon The Earl of Airlie for contributing a Foreword to this book and to Lady Airlie for helping with the Cortachy photographs and family history.

Photographic credits and sources
Angus District Libraries and Museums, Frontispiece, 24, 25, 26, 30, 31, 33, 34, 36, 46, 50, 52, 53, 65, 66, 77, 78, 79, 81, 85, 87, 91, 92, 106, 112, 113, 119, 122, 123, 129, 139, 140, 142, 143, 145, 147, 148.
The Earl and Countess of Strathmore and Kinghorne, Glamis Castle, 4, 5, 6, 7, 8, 9, 10, 40, 45, 49, 67, 73, 83, 84.
Mrs M Irvin, 11, 12, 13, 14, 15, 16, 17.
National Trust for Scotland, (Barrie's Birthplace) 18, 19, 20, 21, 23.
Glenesk Folk Museum, 27, 37, 39, 68, 69, 70, 74, 75, 76, 108, 131.
National Trust for Scotland, (Angus Folk Museum) 29, 42, 48, 57, 120.
Miss Margaret Bruce, Kirriemuir, 22.
Jim Russell, Broughty Ferry, 28, 51, 61, 62, 80, 88, 136.
The Earl and Countess of Airlie, Cortachy Castle, 1, 2, 3, 32, 59, 60, 64, 82, 93, 94.
The High School of Dundee, 41.
The Arbroath Herald, 35, 38, 43, 44, 47, 55, 63, 71, 117, 118, 130, 134, 137, 138, 146.
C P Milligan, 54, 100, 101, 102, 103.
Ian Strachan, 58, 141.
Swallow Hotel, Invergowrie, 110.
George Smith, Arbroath, 56, 126, 132, 133.
City of Dundee District Council, Central Library, 86, 89, 90, 95, 96, 97, 98, 99, 104, 105, 111, 114, 115, 116, 121, 124, 125.
Rev C W Miller, 107.
Mrs and Mrs T Miller, 109.
The Library, University of Dundee, 127, 128, 135, 144.
Ms Elsie Greig, 72.
The Acknowledgements herein, in themselves, constitute a useful research tool as to where quality collections are housed.
RAYMOND LAMONT-BROWN, and PETER ADAMSON

FOREWORD

By The Rt. Hon. The Earl of Airlie, KT, GCVO, DL

ANGUS is surely one of the loveliest counties in Scotland with its varied and beautiful countryside combining its hills and glens with the rolling uplands of the Sidlaws, the inland straths and the long coastal plain.

Its native people are equally varied in their activities which include agriculture, industry and field sports, the combination of which gives the county a very special character.

This book portrays pictorially some of the character and beauty of this part of Scotland and I am proud of the fact that for several centuries my family have played a leading rôle in its political, economic, social and cultural development.

Amateur photography was a relatively rare pursuit in the Victorian and Edwardian times and I was delighted, therefore, to be asked, among others, to provide some family photographs depicting scenes of that period.

I hope readers will feel that the photographs in this book provide an interesting insight into the lives of some of the people of Angus including those of some of my family, their friends and their neighbours.

Cortachy Castle
Kirriemuir
Angus

Frontispiece

A fun-fair on the site of St Ninian's Square, Brechin, 10 July 1883. A farmer walks home with a recently purchased cow. Such fairs began as medieval feasts and occasions for selling livestock and trade goods. They evolved into social gatherings and attracted entertainers of all sorts. Holidays developed in Victorian times; first came Saturday half-holidays, then early-closing days; the 1871 Bank Holiday Act underlined the trend towards commercial holidays, first without pay and then with pay.

VICTORIAN AND EDWARDIAN ANGUS
FROM RARE PHOTOGRAPHS

INTRODUCTION

ALL across the county Hogmanay had been celebrated at midnight. Church bells had rung the length and breadth of Angus from Arbroath to Ardler, and from Edzell to Carnoustie. The old songs had been sung and there was dancing and revelry in the merkat squares and cobbled streets. In the shadows of churches as diverse as the medieval cathedral at Brechin and the then new South Parish Church at Kirriemuir, the pious had stood around and watched the old year out with anticipation. For it was the end as well as the beginning not only of a new year but of a new age.

As the hubbub of the carousers died away the big towns for the most part slumbered in quietness. But down by Easthaven the shoreline was a strand of seaweedy smells and activity, fitfully lit by the masked flares of hurricane lamps. An unexpected catch had been brought in and it had to be unloaded quickly and quietly before the gaugers were abroad.

Dawn came slowly out of the German Ocean, and crept up Tay, Lunan and Esk. It trickled into the sea basin at Montrose and lighted the crowded masts of ships at anchor. It caught the towers of kirk and tollbooth and rolled quietly over the slumbering houses of merchant and fisherman, farmer and weaver. The dawn rolled west across the fields of Strathmore and the waters of Lintrathen and flooded the moors and glens of Angus. A new year – 1837 – had been born. It was a particular moment in history which was to transform the whole county and the people went about their business unaware of the momentous dawning.

As a historical signpost the Victorian Age began at twelve minutes past two on the morning of 20 June 1837 when the last fitful spark of life was finally extinguished from the body of H.R.H. Prince William Henry, the third son of King George III and Queen Charlotte, who had ruled for seven years as King William IV. He was succeeded by his niece, Georgina Charlotte Augusta Alexandrina Victoria, the only daughter of H.R.H. Prince Edward, Duke of Kent and his wife, Her Serene Highness Mary Louisa Victoria of Saxe-Coburg-Saalfeld.

To the people of Angus the only thing that was interesting was that the new monarch was a woman, the first for one hundred and twenty-three years. Her pedigree was not overwhelming. The poet Percy Bysshe Shelley had described William IV and his brothers....whom Victoria called her 'wicked uncles'....as 'the dregs of their dull race' and posterity was not to rescue them from that opinion. Yet, if all other monarchs are forgotten posterity will remember Victoria. Her reign was to last for 64 years. When she came to the throne at nineteen years old the Angus newspapers had recorded that Britain had overcome the greatest power in Europe and was poised for a remarkable expansion of national achievement and wealth. Victoria was to rule over the most powerful nation ever known on earth and she was to give her name to a culture, an era and the highest military decoration that the country could bestow. At the end of her reign she ruled over a global empire 'on which the sun never sets'.

The Victorian Age did not begin all at once, the influences of past decades remained for a long time in Angus, particularly architecturally. By Queen Victoria's day the characteristic features of the Angus landscape were well defined from its mountain background of glens, inland straths and the rolling uplands of the Sidlaws, to the long coastal plain. Through this land had flowed a kaleidoscope of influences from the legionaries of Gnaeus Julius Agricola to the lifestyles of the sea fishing families. From all of these influences there was created a society with a character very much its own. The camera can help us piece together the life and times of the people of Angus during 1837-1910 in a way that no other medium can attempt.

It may be remembered too that long after the Archbishop of Canterbury crowned Victoria Queen on 28 June 1838 many folk still called the county by its old name – Forfarshire. In 1928 the *Scottish Geographical Magazine* was to report that the county of Forfarshire had changed its name officially to Angus. The whole district had originally been an important part of the Pictish confederation known as the province of *Circhenn*, and around the 8th century it was divided into the provinces of Angus and Mearns. Angus incidentally was one of the seven original Earldoms *(Mormaerships)* of Scotland which were feudalised in a process begun in the 12th century. The first nobleman on record to hold the title of Earl *(Comes)* of Angus, as noted by George Edward Cokayne, Clarenceux King of Arms (1900), was one Dufugan who was witness to a charter of *circa* 1114. In time the title was assumed by the heirs of the Douglas family and was merged (but never officially allowed) with the Dukedom of Hamilton.

The county appeared on John Leslie, Bishop of Ross's map in the 16th century as Angus, but on the map within the *System of Geography* (1733), Forfarshire was written on the chart and the text stated: 'Though 'tis called Angus and by the genuine Scots *Aneia*, yet in the rolls of Parliament 'tis named the shire of Forfar'. Again in John Ainslie's map of 1794 it was detailed as the 'County of Forfar or Shire of Angus'; Angus applied to the area as a province (*cf* Buchan or Galloway), but the county was governed under the name of Forfar from the 11th century. In Victorian and Edwardian references both titles are still used to describe the county.

During her sixty-four year reign Queen Victoria's visits to Angus were few, except to pass through the county on her regular pilgrimages to Balmoral. She made her first visit to Angus on Wednesday, 11 September 1844 with Prince Albert and one of her children, Victoria, the Princess Royal. Queen Victoria's royal steam yacht, the *Victoria and Albert*, was met by the *Perth* of the Dundee, Perth and London Shipping Co, to be led through the intricate channel of the Tay. Salutes were fired from Carnoustie and Broughty Ferry. The royal party was greeted by the linen draper George Duncan who had been MP for Dundee since 1841, and Provost Alexander Lawson. On Tuesday, 1 October the royal entourage entered Angus again to return home aboard the royal yacht from Dundee, after their visit to Perthshire.

Victoria was to comment again on Angus and Dundee on her way home from Balmoral in 1879. She recorded in *More Leaves from the Journal of our Life in the Highlands* (1884), 'we....passed again close to the sea by Arbroath, East Haven, Carnoustie....all lying low, with golf links near each, and the line passing over long grass strips with mounds and small indentations of the sea, such as are seen near sands, where there are no rocks and the coast is flat; but the ground rises as you approach Dundee.' Victoria, of course, was describing the route of the Aberdeen/Dundee railway which the Caledonian Railway Co had taken over in 1866 from the Scottish North Eastern Railway; a link with Aberdeen had been established by 1848. The queen continued in her *Journal*: 'We reached the Tay Bridge station at six. Immense crowds were everywhere, flags waving in every direction, and the whole population out; but one's heart was too sad for anything'. Victoria was mourning the death of Louis

1. Queen Victoria and Prince Albert at Osborne House, Isle of Wight, 1859. Osborne was designed by Prince Albert in the Italian style and was completed in 1851. More than any other sovereign, Queen Victoria epitomises the greatness of the British Empire and monarchy.

2. H.R.H. Albert Edward, Prince of Wales, in 1858 at the age of 17, the year he went up to Oxford. As King Edward VII he was to be renowned as a sportsman, a *bon viveur* and lover of beautiful women.

Napoleon, only child of Emperor Napoleon III and the Empress Eugenie. He had been killed a few days before in the Zulu War. Victoria noted: 'Janie Ely *[she was the Marchioness of Ely, Lady of the Bedchamber]*....showed us a Dundee paper, called the *Evening Telegraph*, which contained the fullest and most dreadful accounts. Monstrous!'

The Queen had more to say too about the 1879 stop: 'The Provost, splendidly attired, presented an address. Ladies presented beautiful bouquets to Beatrice *[Princess Beatrice, Victoria's youngest daughter and companion]* and me....We stopped here about five minutes, and then began going over the marvellous Tay Bridge, which is rather more than a mile and a half long. It was begun in 1871. There were great difficulties in laying the foundation, and some lives were lost. It was finished in 1878....Mr Bouch, who was presented at Dundee, was the engineer. It took us, I should say, about eight minutes going over. The view was very fine.' Alas, because of poor workmanship and the lack of allowance for wind-pressure, a great gale struck the bridge on 28 December 1879 and the bridge collapsed as a train was crossing with the loss of about seventy-five lives. The rail link was not constructed again across the Tay until 1882-87.

Victoria's mention of the *Evening Telegraph* (first published in March 1877) underlines the fact that her subjects in Angus were very well-informed. By the beginning of her reign *The Dundee Advertiser* (first issued 16 January 1801) was well established and was under the editorship of Sir John Leng from 1852 to 1906. *The Advertiser* emerged as a powerful voice in local and national politics. In 1861 it became a daily newspaper and ran alongside, and in competition with, the *Dundee Courier* (first issued 20 September 1816). The *Courier* was amalgamated with the *Daily Argus* in 1861, and was firmly under the management of D C Thomson & Co Ltd from 1905. Other papers served the people of Angus, ranging from the *Forfar Herald* (1879) to the *Forfar Review & Strathmore Advertiser* (1888). Several burghs like Arbroath *(Arbroath Argus*, 1835) and Montrose *(Montrose Chronicle*, 1819) sported a wide range of local newspapers and political and critical journals.

During her 'Second Great Expedition' of 1861, Queen Victoria and Prince Albert, with Princess Alice and her fiancé, Prince Louis of Hesse, and attended by Lady Jane Churchill (Lady of the Bedchamber) and General the Hon Charles Grey (Private Secretary to Prince Albert), entered Angus again. They were met at the border of his 'March' by the 11th Earl of Dalhousie, the ex-Secretary for War, and in his company descended from Aberdeenshire into Glen Mark. They drank from the 'White Well' and thereafter the well was called 'The Queen's Well' with the inscription (now vandalised): 'Rest traveller, on this lonely green, and drink and pray for Scotland's Queen'. The party inspected the ruined 16th century Invermark Castle and were entertained at Lord Dalhousie's shooting lodge described by Queen Victoria as 'a new and very pretty house'; their hostess was Miss Maule (later Lady C Maule). After driving and walking along the Northesk they left the county for Fettercairn.

Glen Mark's re-dubbed well was just one of the thousands of 'monuments' which sprang up out of Victorian and Edwardian sentimentality. On Camustane Hill, above the coastal plain that stretches between Monifieth and Carnoustie, for instance, there is the 'Panmure Testimonial', a round tower of 1839, erected to the memory of the Lord Panmure of the day 'by a grateful tenantry'. Montrose favoured political heroes and has its statue (1852) to the Conservative Prime Minister, Sir Robert Peel, and another (1859) in honour of its own Radical MP and supporter of political reform, Joseph Hume.

From the Reform Bill of 1832 to the dissolution of parliament in 1950, Arbroath, Brechin, Forfar, Inverbervie and Montrose formed a constituency known as The Montrose District of Burghs. The rest of the county was the constituency of Forfarshire, and Dundee had its own MPs. For the most part during Victoria and Edward's reigns only those who had the privilege of property could vote so that most folk in Angus had no direct say in who should govern them.

During 1832-1910 the burghs of the Montrose division returned seven Liberal MPs, including some famous names like the celebrated sportsman, Horatio Ross of Rossie Castle, and the aforementioned Joseph Hume who made a fortune in the Honourable East India Company. Within the same period the constituency of Forfarshire was firmly in the hands of the old Whig aristocracy whose families influenced the voting and supplied the candidates for election. The great families were represented by such as Adam Duncan-Haldane, who succeeded as the Earl of Camperdown, and Admiral John Frederick Gordon-Hallyburton of the family of the Marquis of Huntly. By and large the Angus Tory vote was traditionally weak (although the party had aristocratic supporters too like the Earl of Strathmore and Kinghorne), and only one Conservative sat for Forfarshire, namely Major the Hon Charles Maule Ramsay, uncle of the Earl of Dalhousie.

Following the Reform Bill of 1832 Dundee was allocated one MP, the radical reformer George S Kinloch winning the seat for the Liberals. Parliamentary reformers had fought hard in Dundee for their own representation since 1819; formerly Dundee had been grouped with the burghs of Forfar, Perth, Cupar and St Andrews. When Victoria came to the throne, Dundee was represented by Sir Henry Parnell. The Liberals held sway in Dundee during the whole of Victoria and Edward's reigns. After 1868 there were two seats in Dundee, again held by the Liberals. In fact the constituency was rarely fought by the Conservatives (twice in over 50 years) with Liberals fighting Liberals (as in the rest of Angus) under various guises from the Home Rule Liberals to the Liberal Unionists. In the new parliament of 1906 Alexander Wilkie won a seat in Dundee for Labour, and in 1908 he was joined by (the then Liberal) Rt Hon Winston Leonard Spencer Churchill to represent the city. In the year that Edward VII died, Churchill was Home Secretary.

In her memoirs Mabell, Countess of Airlie, who died in 1956, mentions some interesting social rivalries between the Whigs and Tories in Angus, particularly in the use of vocabulary. Lady Airlie said that only the Tories said 'coffee' the Whigs said 'cawfee', and 'yaller' for yellow. 'Orspital' and 'orficer' were the norm in Whig society as was 'napern' for apron. 'To call a chimney piece a mantle piece', said Lady Airlie, 'proclaimed a Tory of deepest dye'.

In terms of local government, up to the Local Government (Scotland) Act of 1889, Angus was administered by a number of local authority and *ad hoc* committees and boards, from the Parish Councils to Boards of Control, to the School Boards and the Commissioners of Supply. In 1889 the new Act consolidated all the local government needs in the county within the County Council and after 1900 the Town Council became the local authority within the burgh for most civic purposes.

Education in Angus was greatly reorganised by the passing of the Education (Scotland) Act, 1872, wherein every parish and burgh in the county had its elected School Board (some 60 in all for the county) for the direction of education for children 'who might otherwise have grown up in ignorance and been nurtured in vice.' In his report for 1875 HM Inspector of Schools, Mr A Dey, found in Angus 'the majority of people exulting in high anticipations of

3.   In this photograph taken by Dr E. Becker, Prince Albert's librarian, on 24 May 1854, Queen Victoria's 35th birthday, the Royal Family are posed in front of the fountain at Osborne House. *L. to R.*: The Prince of Wales, the Princess Royal, Princess Alice, (*in front*) Prince Arthur, Prince Albert, Queen Victoria, Princess Louise, the Duchess of Kent (*Queen Victoria's mother*), Princess Helena and Prince Alfred.

13

the benefits to accrue from the Education Act. . .' One of the immediate tasks of the School Boards was to 'regularise' the school system, build extra schools and enforce attendance as far as possible. To pay for all this there was a charge on parents of around 3d (1p) a week, but after the further Education Act of 1890 elementary education in Angus was virtually 'free'. . . that is it came out of the local rate levied for education.

Up to the 1872 Act the schools of Angus had been divided into Parish Schools, Burgh Schools, Adventure Schools, Private Schools, Schools of Industry and Infant Schools. From long before the Reformation men and women had established 'adventure' schools, so called because they were a financial 'adventure'; the schools were run by many who had only a smattering of education themselves. It was not unusual for tradesmen, from cobblers to public-house keepers, to run a school to augment their income and the majority of poor children up to the 1800s received their education from these establishments (often in dilapidated hovels). Such an Adventure School was located in the Vennel (Nursery Lane), Brechin.

For young ladies and gentlemen of the middle class and the gentry there were the Private Schools run by many an untrained 'Dame' or 'Gentleman of Letters'. The advertisement in the *Montrose Review* (1834) for Miss Henry's School, High Street, Arbroath gives a flavour of the intention: the advert noted that girls were instructed 'in every branch of Useful and Ornamental Education'. It must be remembered though, that, by and large, the education of females during this period was desultory, which contributed a main obstacle to the emancipation of women. Lady Airlie, for instance, remembered that when Lady Kinnaird married at seventeen, her husband was so ashamed at her lack of knowledge that he engaged a governess for her.

Schools of Industry, fundamentally for the instruction of apprentices in their trades, had been extant since monastic times, but in the 19th century they were often a way to feed needy children and keep them out of mischief (the Victorian residents of Angus were much taken with attempts to suppress juvenile delinquency). Another name for these schools was 'Soup-Kitchen Schools' and from 1842 factory children in Dundee were catered for in the Dundee School of Industry. The process went on after the 1872 Act as, for instance, the New Industrial School for Girls was opened by Lady Ogilvie Dalgliesh in 1896. Infant Schools, 'to prevent children from acquiring bad habits and in an attempt to prohibit the prostitution of their puny bodies' were established in such places as Arbroath (1831), Brechin (1837) and Glamis (1836).

Adult education for the masses was expanded by the inauguration of the Mechanics Institutes. These developed from the foundation of Anderson's Institution in Glasgow. John Anderson, a professor at Glasgow University, started evening classes in 1760, and, at his death, left an endowment for the foundation of an adult education college. The basic idea was to bring books and learning skills to the workingclass. In practice, however, the emergent Mechanics Institutes were taken over by the lower middle class for their own entertainment and enlightenment by way of the fact that they were more literate than the workingclass and the lectures and instruction provided was way above the heads of the 'rude mechanicals'.

Around 1870 a movement was also evolved to establish a university in Angus. Between 1870 and 1875 courses of lectures for adults were established in various literary and scientific subjects in Dundee and Angus locations; and, in 1883 there grew University College in Dundee motivated mainly through the public spirited actions of the Baxter family of Balgavies.

With the coming of a new monarch in 1901 the state and status of children began to change. The Education (Scotland) Act of 1908 gave much wider powers to the School Boards, which were now permitted to provide for the medical examination of children at school. The Boards were empowered too, to take legal action against parents whose children were 'unable to profit fully from their education' through neglect. The Act further compelled the attendance of children between the ages of 5 and 14.

Attitudes to children were, however, slow to change and while the children of the upper middle class were well fed and clothed (compared with those of the workingclass) they were 'neglected' by their parents in a way which was not curable by law. Children from well-off families were still banished at an early age to boarding schools and their lives were strongly influenced by Anglo-Saxon educational systems which fitted them for a leading rôle in imperial govenment. Indeed many such children knew their servants better than they knew their parents. For workingclass girls work at 14 was the norm, while middle class girls were only rescued from a life of boredom and inactivity by marriage. And if a proposal of marriage were not obtained by a girl by the time she was 20 then a middle class spinster's chances of self-expression and 'happiness' declined rapidly. Marriage during 1837-1910, although placing a woman firmly as second-fiddle to her husband, was the only way that any woman (unless she was exceptional) of any class could approach any form of individuality.

Throughout the period 1837-1910 agriculture was the main source of employment within Angus (outside Dundee). *The New Statistical Account of Scotland* (1845) has its landward correspondents commenting upon innovative schemes of tillage and animal husbandry. For instance the Leicester breed of sheep joined the traditional blackface at such places as Airlie by this time and farmers like Hugh Walton of Kettins parish had won fame outside the county for the breeding of traditional Angus cattle. The county had seen many an agricultural invention too, for Patrick Bell of Mid Leoch in the parish of Auchterhouse had become famous for his reaping machine, first used in 1828.

Such institutions at the Eastern Forfarshire Farming Association (founded 1814) promoted the latest agricultural implements and held annual cattle and husbandry shows. Experiments in large scale farming were conducted in the 1800s at Careston for instance, and these were the days of the steam engine which pulled a ploughshare by wire ropes up and down the fields. When Victoria came to the throne the yearly wage of farm labourers was around £12 'with their meal and milk' for a 60 hour week; by 1910 this had risen to around £100 a year 'including perquisites'. Shepherds and cattlemen were paid overtime for Sunday work.

By 1901 emphasis shifted to agriculture, with forestry and sea fishing. In terms of forestry the Angus-born Professor Mark L Anderson tells in his *History of Scottish Forestry* (1967) that by the coming of Victoria there were 28,000 acres of new woodland in the county. Angus was known for its oaks (at Glamis), its Wellingtonians (at Cortachy) and its beeches, pines and firs (at Lethamgrange).

Today scholars still aver that Auchmithie is probably the oldest fishing village in Angus; in 1840 all the population of 280 earned a living from the fishing industry, and by 1880 there were 33 boats out of this small village. Local landowners like Horatio Ross of Rossie Castle encouraged fishing.

Despite the international importance of Dundee as a whaling port, the shipping trade in Angus was centred on Arbroath and Montrose and was fiercely competitive with Aberdeen and Dundee. When Arbroath was a commercial port large quantities of stone, flax and potatoes were shipped out, and the coal trade gave employment to a large fleet of schooners and brigs. In the 1870s and 1880s the export of seed and ware potatoes (the latter being large potatoes sold for consumption, as opposed to seed potatoes) provided the coastal population of Angus with flourishing employment. The Irish potato famine, 1846-47 and the Franco-Prussian War, 1870-71 contributed a great deal to this trade.

During the 1870s too, Arbroath imported flax from the Baltic by sea. There was a fluctuating trade too in wood and herring. When the Forth Railway Bridge was being built 1883-9, some 330 ships moved stone from Carmyllie Quarry. The peak of Arbroath as a ship-owning port came in the mid-1850s before sail gave way to steam; by the end of the Victorian era Arbroath had ceased as a ship-owning port. The last merchant ship built at Arbroath was the two-masted brigantine *The Macbain*, launched 1881.

Montrose was basically an agricultural port, but it also had a whaling fleet (the port's last and most successful ship was the *Eliza Swan*, sold off in the 1840s). As well as cargoes of flax, coal, herring and potatoes, Montrose ships carried grain from the Black Sea and emigrants to Canada aboard such famous vessels as the *Emigrant* (maiden voyage to the St Lawrence, 1856). Indeed the Baltic trade was at its height in Montrose in the 1850s. Iron ship-building was introduced in the 1870s.

One enormous change for the county during Victorian and Edwardian times was in terms of transport. In 1837 the horse was still supreme and four-wheeled wooden wagons and two-wheeled carts, all with iron-rimmed wooden wheels, were the most common forms of road haulage. Horses yoked to ploughs and leisurely cutting straight furrows was a sight that caused little attention and every farm-worker was expected to know the basics of horse grooming and the routine of the stable. Whole communities depended on the horse and even in such small parishes as Careston the smithy regularly shoed 100 pairs of horses. The invention of the steam engine began the decline of horse transport.

A pioneer railway in the county was the Dundee and Newtyle track incorporated 26 May 1826; passenger services commenced on 16 December 1831 between the Law of Dundee and Hatton Hill, near Newtyle. A fare of 1/6d (7½p) for an inside seat was charged and 1/- (5p) for one open to the elements; the eleven mile journey took 1¼ hours. Of the opening journey the *Perthshire Courier* remarked: 'passengers were highly gratified with their ride and we understand that, in ascending and descending the inclined plane at Balbeuchly, no great difference of motion was felt, nor any alarm excited, the slope being so gradual as to occasion no disagreeable sensation'.

The Dundee and Arbroath and the Arbroath and Forfar Railways were undoubtedly the product of the foresight and resolution of such as landowner, William Lindsay Carnegie (Arbroath and Forfar Railway) and steam power enthusiast, Lord Kinnaird (Dundee and Perth Railway). So by 1850 all the main railway routes had linked every major town in Angus and up to the 1920s the railways had a virtual monopoly of the county's heavy traffic.

Railway construction relandscaped many an Angus horizon and right up to the end of the century burgh architecture was enhanced by the building of handsome stations. Brechin station, for instance, originally built in 1847-48 as the terminus of the line from Montrose, and remodelled in 1894-95, was a fine example of the new building fashions.

Yet, by far the largest amount of building during Victorian and Edwardian times was in the field of domestic architecture. Panbride House (1856), near Carnoustie, and Kinnettles (1867), near Forfar, are fine examples of the skills of the period. Successful manufacturers and merchants too were spending money to build houses on the outskirts of the towns and many of them vied with each other for splendour. In his entertaining autobiography *My*

16

Scottish Youth (1937), the diplomatist and writer, Sir Robert H. Bruce Lockhart (1887-1970) had this to say about these merchants' expectations and building rivalries in the burgeoning Victorian and Edwardian Broughty Ferry: '. . . the jute merchants of Dundee . . . were careful spenders, but had fine houses built of stone and situated in the best residential area on the spur of the hills overlooking the sea. A stone mansion was solid, and solidity, both financial and moral, was the summit of their ambitions. Building was therefore the only temptation which led to extravagances, and before our arrival *[1890s]* there had been a great architectural competition between two wealthy jute families, the Grimonds and the Gilroys. In our time the Gilroys were very much on top, for the Grimonds' place was in the town, and had little land round it, and was, I think, unoccupied, while the Gilroys had a magnificent fortress, which bore the historic sounding name of Castle Roy, on the crest of the highest hill'.

Just as the beginning of Victoria's reign had been a historical watershed, the coming of her son Edward's reign was another important turning point. The Edwardian Age began in the wake of tremendous change. By the time Queen Victoria died at 6.30pm on 22 January 1901 at Osborne House, Isle of Wight, Britain had lost her supremacy in foreign commerce. In the year of Edward VII's coronation two events were to have great significance. On 13 July 1902 the Conservative Prime Minister, Lord Salisbury, resigned and after a decade out of office the Liberals were given a mandate to try to satisfy the needs of the people. Their task was great; increasing unemployment was bringing with it hunger and social discontent. On 30 January 1902 the signing of a treaty of alliance between Britain and Japan underlined the end of that 'splendid isolation' which had been Britain's international rôle since the Crimean War.

Rich and poor alike looked to Edward VII's reign with great optimism. Many believed that Edward should have come to the throne ten years earlier. The Boer War – the worst war Britain had ever suffered, with over 100,000 casualties, was conducted by an army that was half-starved at times – ended on 31 May 1902 and the nation wanted to forget. Their new king, attractive and avuncular, was to give them public splendour and colour after his mother's largely grey court. Edward had the confidence of the country's youth who believed that he would do away with what they regarded as the false morality, hypocritical behaviour and hollow ideas of the Victorian era.

But the hope and confidence was to be shortlived. When Edward VII died at Buckingham Palace on 6 May 1910 the seemingly ordered, prosperous and sunny days of his reign were to become only a nostalgic memory. Four years later Britain's ebullient youth was to be slaughtered in the mud of the Franco-Belgian frontier.

CHAPTER ONE

GLAMIS CASTLE AND THE BOWES LYON FAMILY

4.   The entrance front, Glamis Castle, incorporating the East Wing of 1891, constructed by Claude, the 13th Earl of Strathmore and Kinghorne. The clock dates from 1811. The photograph was taken before the walls and gateway of the Dutch Garden were set out under the East Wing.

GLAMIS Castle is the home of the Bowes Lyon family and the seat of the Earls of Strathmore and Kinghorne. The castle has been inhabited by descendants of the Lyon family since 1372, when Sir John Lyon, Keeper of the Privy Seal, was granted the thanage of Glamis by King Robert II, the first Stewart King of Scotland. In 1376 Sir John married Robert II's daughter, the Princess Joanna.

During the 15th century the Lyon family continued to play a prominent rôle in Scotland's government and in 1445 Patrick Lyon of Glamis was created a peer in Parliament with the title of Lord Glamis. This led to his being made a Lord of Session in 1457 and finally Master of the Royal Household. For decades the family prospered as courtiers, but on 14 July 1537, Janet Douglas, Lady Glamis, was burned for witchcraft at Edinburgh Castle, and Glamis became forfeit to the Crown. On the death of James V, the castle and estate of Glamis were restored to the young Lord Glamis. In 1606 the then Lord Glamis was created Earl of Kinghorne. The title was further developed in 1677 when it was restyled as the Earldom of Strathmore and Kinghorne; the recipient of this new title, Patrick Lyon, proceeded to alter and enlarge the castle and make many improvements. Today the pinky-grey stone soaring edifice of rounded towers, conical turrets and battlements is the work of many generations each transforming it from the original tower-house into a distinctive castle.

Glamis, in the Vale of Strathmore, was long a royal hunting lodge and its royal associations date from very early times. Malcolm II died in or near Glamis on 25 Nov 1034 and following the death of Lady Glamis in 1537, King James V and his Queen, Marie de Guise-Lorraine, held court in the castle (and purloined most of its treasures). Their daughter Mary, Queen of Scots, dined and slept at Glamis on her way to quell the Huntly rebellion, and her son, James VI was also a frequent visitor. Another royal prince who held court here was James Francis Edward Stuart, the 'Old Pretender'. He lodged in the castle in 1716 during the illfated rebellion to restore the Stuarts to the British throne. The castle was the childhood home of Her Majesty Queen Elizabeth The Queen Mother, and on 21 August 1930 Her Royal Highness The Princess Margaret Rose, grand-daughter of the 14th Earl, was born in the castle.

The first decades of the 19th century saw great improvements at Glamis, for now the Strathmores were in residence most of the time after a generation of living on their estates in Yorkshire and Hertfordshire. Important structural changes were carried out in 1811 by John, 10th Earl (d.1820). The castle clock dates from 1811. During October 1866 the castle's chapel was re-opened for Divine Service. This Episcopal chapel had been first opened and consecrated in 1688.

In 1891 a wing of baronial style was built on to the existing 17th century wing at the east end of Glamis which now incorporates the private residence of the present Earl and Countess and their family; this construction was the work of Claude, the 13th Earl (d.1904) who also had the plaster ceiling added to the castle's Billiard Room to celebrate his golden wedding. Much repair and preservation work was carried out by Claude George, the 14th Earl. Outside, the Dutch Garden was set out by the 13th Earl who had a formal sunken garden laid out below the East Wing. Between 1907-10 the Italian Garden was completed to the design of Countess Cecilia, helped by the Head Gardener, Thomas Wilson. The modern nature trail exhibits a red cedar presented to the Strathmores by Her Royal Highness Princess Louise, Marchioness of Lorne, and planted in March 1893.

5.   Captain Oswald Ames, 2nd Life Guards and Patrick, Master of Glamis, 1890. In the centre of the picture is the famous baroque sundial with its four main facets and unique 'pineapple' top with 84 miniature dials; placed here by Patrick, 3rd Earl, between 1671 and 1680. The site was calculated to be three degrees west of the Meridian at Greenwich.

6.   Lady Elizabeth Bowes Lyon and the Hon David Bowes Lyon in the Drawing Room at Glamis, 1909. In this Lafayette portrait, Lady Elizabeth is wearing a rose-pink and silver dress made for her by Countess Cecilia; the style is that of James VI & I's daughter who was later to be the Winter Queen of Bohemia. The Hon David is wearing a parti-coloured costume depicting the family jester, with cap and bells, a treasure of the dressing-up chest. In these costumes the children danced and entertained guests at Glamis. Mrs Thompson, the housekeeper at Glamis from 1886 to 1915 wrote thus to Lady Cynthia Asquith; 'They were the dearest little couple I have ever seen . . . . I remember Lady Elizabeth inviting me to play cricket with them. She had great fun at me as I could not send the ball anywhere near the wicket. She was a merry child and always friendly.'

7. Lady Elizabeth Angela Marguerite Bowes Lyon and her brother the Hon David Bowes Lyon at Glamis. On 23 April 1923, Lady Elizabeth married His Royal Highness Albert Frederick Arthur George, Duke of York, the second son of King George V and later to reign as King George VI. The Hon David had been born in 1902 and during World War I was sent to Washington to take over the political warfare and propaganda work of British Security Co-ordination. As the Hon Sir David Bowes Lyon he died in 1961 while staying with his sister at Birkhall. Countess Cecilia had called her two youngest children 'My Benjamins'. Of his sister the Hon Sir David remembered: 'She was very quick at learning and always left me far behind to the despair of the teachers.'

8. A family portrait outside the front entrance, Glamis Castle, 1892. Claude, 13th Earl of Strathmore is seated holding the hand of his grandson, Patrick, then Master of Glamis; he was the Queen Mother's eldest brother, and became the 15th Earl in 1944. Standing is Claude, Lord Glamis, who was the Queen Mother's father; he became the 14th Earl in 1904.

9. The seven sons of the 13th Earl of Strathmore pose out-
    side the main entrance to Glamis Castle, 1886. *L. to R.:*
    (Back Row) Ernest (1858-91), HM Diplomatic Service;
    Patrick (1863-1946), Barrister; Kenneth (1867-1911).
    (Middle Row): Claude George, Lord Glamis (1855-
    1944), Lt 2nd Life Guards; Francis (1856-1948), Col
    Black Watch; Herbert (1860-97), Barrister; *(Front):*
    Malcolm (1874-1957), Lt Col Black Watch.

10. Lady Elizabeth Bowes Lyon on her pony outside the entrance front of Glamis Castle. One visitor to Glamis recalled to
    Lady Cynthia Asquith: 'She was an extraordinarily graceful, dainty, engaging child.'

CHAPTER TWO

THE TAY RAILWAY BRIDGE, 1887

ON Sunday, 28 December 1879, part of the first Tay Railway Bridge fell into the river at the height of a great storm which measured Force 8-9 on the Beaufort scale. It took with it a north-bound train. The final death toll was estimated at seventy-five, but fewer than fifty bodies were recovered from the Tay. At the subsequent enquiry, chaired by Henry Cadogan Rothery, Commissioner for Wrecks, the bridge's designer, Sir Thomas Bouch, was declared negligent (on a minority verdict) for not making sufficient allowance for wind pressure. The foundation stone for this railway bridge had been laid in 1871 and the first train had crossed from Wormit to Dundee in 1877.

Some six months after the disaster, the North British Railway (Tay Bridge) Bill brought before Parliament the problem of re-building the rail-link between Fife and Angus. In November 1881 the North British Railway Company gave the work for a new bridge to Messrs Arrol & Co, Glasgow. Contruction began in June 1882.

The second Tay Railway Bridge was sited some sixty feet upstream of its predecessor's still visible wrecked piers and consisted of 85 iron spans to a length of 2 miles 364 yards; seventy-four spans are over the waterway. The new bridge, designed by William Barlow, was built at a cost of £640,000.

The bridge was opened to goods traffic on Monday, 13 June 1887, and the first train across was a heavy goods at 1300 hours from Dundee to Bothwell Junction; the bridge was opened for passenger traffic later the same month. The bridge remains the longest railway bridge in the United Kingdom.

11. No 16 pontoon for lifting girders, 18 May 1886. The work boats and plant are seen shifting the old 129ft and 145ft girders from the old to the new piers. Girders from the original bridge were incorporated into the new bridge, as outside girders in the approach spans.

12. Brick arching and wrought iron superstructure Wormit side. The spans on staging, in the process of construction, are seen in the centre of the picture. Each span weighed in excess of 500 tons and was 245 ft long. From the workyard at Wormit, men and machinery were carried over the old bridge.

13. Deck of construction pontoon showing excavators for dredging and sinking the cylinders for the bridge foundation, 9 March 1886. These pontoons were constructed with a platform on telescopic supports, so that the height could be varied to suit the levels of work and the bearing of the girders.

14. As a part of the new construction the old 70ft girders of the original bridge were transferred to the new piers. Here the girders are brought out by traverses, 3 March 1886. In the background is the line of the Dundee & Perth Railway (Caledonian) and the Dundee foreshore before the Esplanade Extension.

15. Towing the 245ft spans across the Tay. A feature of the construction was the use of 'Arrol's Quadrupeds', pontoons to carry machinery capable of sinking the caissons. The pontoons were supported on legs which rested on the bed of the Tay. It took twenty-one days to lift each span 77ft to its final resting place on top of the piers.

16. The 245 ft spans end on to the line of the bridge, being turned into position at the piers, 21 May 1886. The spans were towed into place by three paddle steamers of which two are seen on the far right of the picture.

17. The Tay Railway Bridge from the Fife side showing the first passenger train crossing 20 June 1887. A pontoon still remains in position by the brick arching on the Wormit side. The subsequent development of the village of Wormit was influenced by the re-opening of the bridge.

CHAPTER THREE

SIR JAMES MATTHEW BARRIE AND KIRRIEMUIR

JAMES Matthew Barrie was born on 9 May 1860 at Lilybank in the Tenements, 9 Brechin Road, Kirriemuir, then still a small weaving town, some five miles north-west of Forfar. His parents were David Barrie, weaver, and Margaret Ogilvy, the daughter of a stonemason, (following the Scottish custom of the time, she kept her maiden name after marriage). They had married in 1841 and had ten children; James Matthew was their ninth child.

Barrie first attended the 'dame' school set up by the Misses Adam in Bank Street and thence the school attached to the South Free Kirk at Southmuir. On 19 August 1868 Barrie was entered as a pupil of Glasgow Academy, where his elder brother was Classical Master.

The family moved from the Tenements, Brechin Road to the Limepots (now Canmore Street), Forfar, in 1870 when David Barrie became a clerk at Laird's Linen Works. James Matthew Barrie now entered Forfar Academy. Two years later David Barrie was moved to Laird's new factory in Kirriemuir, and rented the upper portion of a villa called Strathview. The Barrie family were later to occupy the whole house, and Barrie's parents and sister Jane Ann died there. The wedding ceremony of Barrie and the actress Mary Ansell took place at Strathview on 9 July 1894 conducted by Barrie's uncle Dr David Ogilvy.

While still at Forfar Academy Barrie began to write stories and saw a life of literature as his aim. It was from his mother's fireside tales and everyday comments on Kirriemuir's inhabitants and their customs that Barrie drew the bulk of his early inspiration. Soon he was to rejoin his brother Alexander at Dumfries; and thence attended the Academy. At this time only holidays meant residence at Kirriemuir. While at Dumfries Barrie tried his hand at playwriting.

In 1878 James Matthew Barrie entered Edinburgh University and again Kirriemuir was only a place where he spent vacations. Barrie graduated MA in 1882 and there followed a period of freelance writing in Edinburgh. Then he moved to Nottingham to work on the local newspaper. Yet, to Barrie the literary mecca of the age was London and he moved there in 1884.

18. James Barrie's birthplace, the Tenements, 9 Brechin Road, Kirriemuir, 1895. Barrie was born in an upstairs room. Bought soon after Barrie's death in 1937 by D E Alves, the property was gifted to the National Trust for Scotland and it now houses the Barrie Museum.

19. James Barrie's mother, Margaret Ogilvy, with her children, circa 1848. *L. to R.:* Mary (1845-1919), became a teacher and married John Galloway; Jane Anne (1847-95) died unmarried after caring for her mother with loving patience; Alexander (1842-1914), became a prominent educationalist.

Barrie's subsequent career is literary history, but Kirriemuir greatly featured in his success, and his mother's memories dressed up as *Auld Licht Idylls* (1888) was his first real taste of success. And his *A Window in Thrums* (1889) – 'Thrums' being the fictionalised Kirriemuir – put his home town on the map. The Den, a ravine now a public park in Kirriemuir, is mentioned in *Sentimental Tommy* (1896). Barrie's stories of 'Thrums' – a name taken from the bunch of loose threads which hung beside every handloom and which were used to mend broken threads in fabric – engendered a loyal readership. Even so, many of the townsfolk of Kirriemuir did not take kindly to the publicity. Many years were to pass before the folk of Kirriemuir forgave Barrie for making fun, as they saw it, of their deeply held religious beliefs, their customs and habits. Thrums was again the setting for Barrie's *The Little Minister* (1891).

By the time Edward VII became King, world-wide popularity had come to Barrie and wealth poured in on him. His *Peter Pan* (1904) gave him literary immortality. Barrie was created a baronet in 1913 and was awarded the Order of Merit in 1922. He was elected Rector of the University of St Andrews in 1919.

After 1868 Barrie was only an occasional visitor to his birthplace. But he kept alive fond memories of such boyhood chums as Jimmy Robb the Kirriemuir ironmonger, who visited him at his flat in Adelphi Terrace, London. There they recalled days spent fishing and scrambling up the hills. In the summer of 1933 Barrie rented Balnaboth House, in Glen Prosen, for a month and held a house party there. Jimmy Robb and his daughter came to lunch, and a highlight of the summer was a visit to Balnaboth by Their Royal Highnesses the Duke and Duchess of York with Princess Elizabeth and Princess Margaret. The following day

20. Margaret Ogilvy (1819-95), was the daughter of a Kirriemuir stonemason who was a supporter of that fiercely puritanical band of Protestants known as the 'Auld Lichts'. Margaret's reminiscences of these folk gave James Barrie his first literary success. Barrie idolised his mother and wrote her biography in 1896 which still stands today as an interesting insight into Scottish life and character.

Barrie visited Glamis to attend Princess Margaret's third birthday party; she later declared: 'He is my greatest friend and I am *his* greatest friend!

Barrie died on 19 June 1937 and, on his own instructions, his body was conveyed to Kirriemuir and he was buried beside Margaret Ogilvy, his father, sisters and brother David, in the hill cemetery, a short walk away from his birthplace.

In 1928 Barrie's birthplace at 9 Brechin Road was bought by Major R D Lauder. There was consternation in Kirriemuir when a report circulated that the home was to be demolished stone by stone and re-erected as a Barrie Museum in the United States; local feeling was further aroused when a proposal was made to transfer the detached wash-house (where Barrie and Jimmy Robb had staged Barrie's first drama) at Brechin Road, to Kensington Gardens. Yet, shortly after Barrie's death in 1937, Duncan Elliott Alves, of Bryn Bras Castle, Caernarvon, bought the property and handed it over to the National Trust for Scotland. The house was restored after 1961 and the National Trust for Scotland set it out as a museum to house Barrie's personal posessions, mementoes and exhibitions relevant to the author's achievements.

Memories of Barrie are still alive in the recall of Miss Margaret Bruce. Talking in 1986 – then aged 94 – at her home in Elm Street, she remembered her family friendship with the Barries dating from 1904. 'Sir James was a very quiet person and I think he was a very lonely man', she said. 'The Barries were always highly respected in Kirriemuir and they took a great deal of active interest in local affairs.'

21. David Barrie (1814-1902), weaver, was one of the most respected men in Kirriemuir, and a devotee of self-education. He married Margaret Ogilvy in 1841. David Barrie was described by the Rev Alexander Whyte as 'a typical Forfarshire figure of a man; a fine, open, intelligent countenance, the mouth mobile and humoursome, the brows broad and full, and a fringe of whisker framing the face, of which both lip and chin were shaven.'

22. A Barrie family group at Strathview, Southmuir, Kirriemuir, in 1902. *L. to R.:* The Rev Dr David Ogilvy, J M Barrie's uncle. He had resigned the ministry in 1896 and made his home at Strathview with his brother-in-law, David Barrie and his niece Sara; David Barrie, J M Barrie's father, who died in the year the photograph was taken, aged 87; Sara Mitchell Barrie, J M Barrie's sister; she had become a governess at Miss Oliver's School, Rutland Place, Edinburgh, and she died in Nov 1903 aged 49. She had been the housekeeper and adopted daughter of Dr Ogilvy, who outlived the other two in the picture; he died in 1904 aged 82. Strathview – which Barrie always spelled Strath View – had been bought by Dr Ogilvy and was leased to David Barrie. It was to become the home of J M Barrie's brother Alexander Ogilvy Barrie who died there in 1914 at the age of 72.

23. James Barrie at his desk in the study at Strathview, 1 Forfar Road, Kirriemuir, composing *The Little Minister*, circa 1890. Set in 'Thrums', Barrie's fictionalised Kirriemuir, the book was published in 1891 and tells the story of a minister who falls in love with a gypsy girl.

24. As J M Barrie became famous people flocked to Kirriemuir to see the original window immortalised in his book *A Window in Thrums* (1889). To ensure privacy and stop visitors peering in the windows of Strathview, the Barries said that the white cottage opposite, with the little gable window, in Glamis road, was *the* original 'House on the Brae'. In reality it was not.

CHAPTER FOUR

VEHICLES FOR COMMERCE AND PLEASURE

ANGUS 1838-1909: A TRANSPORT CHRONOLOGY

1838	First train travels the Dundee and Arbroath Railway.
	Arbroath and Forfar Railway officially opened.
1841	12 Feb. Steam engines *Britannia* and *Victoria* collide at Clocksbriggs.
1847	Opening of Perth and Dundee Railway.
1847-48	Brechin railway station built as the terminus for the line from Montrose.
1850	1 April. London-Aberdeen through train passes through Strathmore.
1853	Arbroath's sailing fleet reached 119 sailing ships totalling 15,114 tons.
1855	Light railway opened to serve Carmyllie quarries.
1856	The *Emigrant* built by J & D Birnie of Montrose, sails to the St Lawrence.
	The *Neville* of 830 tons, the largest ship ever built in Arbroath.
1861	Alyth and Kirriemuir railway opened.
1865	'Red Flag Act' limits locomotive speed on roads to 4mph (country); 2mph (urban).
	Buddon Ness lighthouse completed by David & Thomas Stevenson.
1866	Scottish North Eastern Railway absorbed by Caledonian Railway.
1869	*TTS Mars* moored in the Tay at the instigation of W E Baxter MP for Montrose.
1870	Scurdie Lighthouse completed by David and Thomas Stevenson.
1873	Dundee whaling fleet comprises ten steamships.
1874	First ship launched from the Caledon yard, Dundee, 178 ton *Ilda*.
1877	26 Sept. First train crosses Tay Bridge.
	Establishment of the lightship *Abertay* at the mouth of the Tay.
1877-98	Dundee Tramway & Carriage Co, operates, then taken over by City.
1878	1 June. Public opening of Tay Bridge.
1879	Tay Bridge Disaster.
1880	Dundee & Arbroath Railway becomes joint line (North British/Caledonian).
1881	Montrose and Bervie railway vested in the North British Railway Co.
	The *MacBain*, a 278-ton brigantine, the last merchant ship built at Arbroath.
1883	Montrose to Arbroath Railway opened. First North British through trains to Aberdeen.
1885	Steam trams introduced to Dundee.
1887	New Tay Railway Bridge opened.
1890	Fifty-four vessels arrive at Montrose with 24,540 tons of goods.
1894-5	Completion of the railway to Forfar and Edzell from Brechin.
1896	Act 'emancipates' motoring; now allowed to reach 12mph.
1900	Electric tramcars introduced by Dundee Corporation Tramways.
1901	Captain R F Scott's ship *Discovery* launched.
1903	Preston A Watson builds bi-plane and test flies at Belmont.
	Compulsory licence plates appear, speed limit raised to 20mph.
1905	Monifieth linked to Dundee by tramway.
	Formation of the Automobile Association.
1906	The only place in Angus where petrol could be bought was Dundee.
1909	Foden steam wagon works out of Forfar.

25. Betsy Leighton of Kirriemuir leans on her bicycle in this studio shot of *circa* 1905. As bicycling became popular, special costumes were designed for the enthusiasts. By 1898 knickerbockers and gaiters were being worn by keen women cyclists, but here Betsy sports her 'Sunday best' rather than a cycling outfit. The drop-frame, which allowed women to mount the machine without throwing a leg indecorously over the saddle did not appear until the 1890s. Betsy Leighton had been born in 1884 at Longbank Farm, Kirriemuir. From the age of fourteen she was employed as a domestic servant on various farms in the Kirriemuir-Forfar area. The bicycle represented many years of saving. According to her daughter, Mrs Mary Carstairs, Betsy averred that she was one of the first women in Kirriemuir to own and ride a bicycle. In 1906 Betsy married John Carstairs, a farm worker; she died in 1972, aged 88.

26. G H Strachan, Arbroath, *circa* 1887, in this studio portrait by Geddes & Son. Strachan was the Sheriff Officer, JP Constable and Town Officer of the burgh and his office was at 1 Hill St, Arbroath. Pedals had been applied to a tricycle by a Dumfriesshire blacksmith called McMillan in 1834. Rubber tyres were introduced in 1868 and pneumatic tyres were 're-invented' for bicycles by J B Dunlop in 1888. The tricycle was popularised by Princess Mary, Duchess of Teck who took to riding one around the royal parks. The Cyclists' Touring Club was founded in 1878.

27. André Letta's Caravan Concert Tourers. This group of entertainers travelled Angus giving open-air concerts. Live entertainment saw its last great heyday in the Edwardian era, when it was eclipsed by the cinema, the wireless and the gramophone. Small purpose-built cinemas developed from around 1908; by 1917 three million people a day were 'going to the pictures' in the United Kingdom.

28. The three-in-hand Clova Mail Coach, pre-1910. The coach provided an important mail and transport link between Milton of Clova, on the River South Esk, and Kirriemuir, Forfar and the south. The print made a popular postcard which was sold by Duncan, Post Office, Clova.

29. Sir James Matthew Barrie's sister-in-law in the 'Victoria' with John the coachman, in Glen Prosen. Beside the carriage is Alec Scoogal, husband of Mrs Barrie's sister. Mrs Mary Barrie had married J M Barrie's brother, Alexander Ogilvy Barrie in 1877; she was the daughter of Cowan the Edinburgh jeweller, and she had two sons and four daughters. She died at Strathview, Kirriemuir, in 1928 aged 72. The elegant English carriage, named for Queen Victoria, was originally a four-wheeled, doorless vehicle, with a forward-facing seat for two covered with a folding, or calash top. There was an elevated coachman's seat for two above the front axle.

30. North British Railway engine 595 and tender at the Wellgate Signal Box, Arbroath, *circa* 1890. The engine was an NBR Class N-Holmes 7ft of the '592' series built at Cowlairs, 1886-87. The design was prepared in anticipation of the re-opening of the Tay Bridge to passenger traffic, 20 June 1887 and the introduction of through working between Burntisland and Aberdeen. The series was rebuilt by Reid in 1911, came into the LNER system and was withdrawn 1926-33.

31. Brechin Station, Caledonian Railway, 1900. The Forfar and Brechin Railway was opened for passenger traffic on 1 June 1895; in 1896 the Brechin and Edzell Railway was opened. The Brechin Agricultural & Trading Co buildings lie to the right, and the coal yards to the left.

32. The Countess of Airlie stands at the old front door of Cortachy Castle with her six children, Lady Kitty, Lady Helen, Lady Mabell, Lord Ogilvy, Hon Bruce and Hon Patrick. The car is a 1902-1903 French CGV model from the Puteaux-based company of Fernand Charron, Leonce Girardot and Emile Voigt. The first CGV had appeared in 1901. The cars always appealed to wealthy sportsmen. As Lady Mabell Frances Elizabeth Gore, the Countess of Airlie was the daughter of the 5th Earl of Arran and had married the 11th Earl of Airlie in 1886. For over fifty years she was lady-in-waiting to Her Majesty Queen Mary.

33. Kalac's Cycle & Motor Depot, Castle St, Forfar in the late years of Edward VII's reign. The depot (now the site of Adamson's booksellers) stood next to the Post Office. The depot proprietor, John Kellacky, sits in the 1907-08 Humber motor car with W G Gibson. The car was the 15 HP model. The number plate is for Dundee Burgh Council. The depot window advertises the popular Swift and Triumph cycles. British bicycles were exported from Birmingham from 1885 by Siegfried Bettmann and in 1886 he changed the name to Triumph. In 1887 the Triumph manufacturing facility was set up at Coventry. The first Triumph motorcycle was manufactured in 1902.

34. Dr Norman J. Sinclair, County Medical Officer of Health for Angus in his 1908-09 Argyll 12/14 HP automobile which had been made at the Alexandria works. The car bears the registration letters for Angus County Council. Doctors were amongst the first professional men to use motor cars and most owners of private motor vehicles belonged either to those who could afford a chauffeur, or a prosperous tradesman with a talent for engineering and who could supervise repairs.

35. Pony and trap with liveried groom outside the Thistle Hotel. Possession of one's own carriage was a mark of social status and in the Victorian age such ownership spread from the upper classes down to the lower middle class, giving rise to the term 'carriage trade' to denote the prosperous.

36. Cabs at Brechin Railway Station, *circa* 1890. These cabs belonged to the various hotels and the cab in the middle is clearly marked Commercial Hotel (now the Northern), Clerk St, Brechin.

37. A coach and four set out at a spanking pace in this photograph from the Glenesk Folk Museum, Tarfside, Brechin. Once a shooting lodge for the Earls of Dalhousie, the museum was opened in 1955 and reflects agricultural, leisure and domestic life in Glenesk. The Glen was much visited by Victorian and Edwardian coaching parties.

38. Employees of Messrs Strachan, Wallace & Whyte, wholesalers of beverages, liquors and groceries, 1900. The photograph was taken, probably just before a 'works outing', at the company's premises at Tower Neuk, 250 High St. Arbroath.

39. The Lochlee-Invermark coach belonging to the Crown Hotel outside the Glenesk Hotel, High Street, Edzell, prepares for an excursion. Invermark Castle, seventeen miles northwest of Edzell, with the nearby deer forest, was a popular venue for Victorian and Edwardian tourists. Many folk in the parish of Lochlee used to let out their homes in summer and move into old houses kept for the purpose.

40. Known as the 'Station 'bus' this carriage sits outside the main entrance to Glamis Castle. The doorway is in the tower begun in the early 17th century by the 1st Earl of Kinghorne, and was completed by the 3rd Earl whose bust within a circular niche appears above the Royal Arms.

CHAPTER FIVE

SCHOOLS AND PUPILS

THE HIGH SCHOOL OF DUNDEE

AROUND the year 1220 a Grammar School was founded in Dundee by the Abbot and Monks of Lindores, under a charter granted by Gilbert, Bishop of Brechin. This charter was confirmed by Pope Gregory IX on 14 February 1239. Among the eminent people educated at the early schools were such as the Scottish patriot Sir William Wallace (c 1274-1305) and the historian and first Principal of Aberdeen University, Hector Boece (c.1465-1536).

After the Reformation the school passed to the administration of the Town Council and in 1589 it received its first permanent home in St Clement's Lane, where it remained until 1789 when the Grammar School moved to School Wynd. There the school shared a building with the English School which had been founded earlier in the century.

In 1829 the two schools were united with Dundee Academy (opened at the Nethergate in 1785) to form the Dundee Public Seminaries in the Meadows. The present school was built to house all three schools, and the new school was opened on 1 October 1834. Within the new building the centre was assigned to the Academy, the west wing to the Grammar School and the east wing to the English School. An overall Rector was not appointed until 1883. The buildings were designed by the distinguished Edinburgh architect, George Angus, in classical style and they cost £10,000. Under a Royal Charter of 1859 the name of the schools was changed to The High School of Dundee

During 1886-90 the Girls' School was built in Euclid Crescent, following the completion of the work-shop (1883-86, one of the first of its kind in Scottish schools) and the gymnasium set behind the main building; this expansion was funded by Baillie William Harris and the gymnasium was equipped at the expense of ex-Provost William Robertson. The original curriculum of the school was drawn up by Robert Bell, a school Director, in 1877. In 1898 the Physics Laboratory was set up, and in 1901 the playing field at Dalnacraig was provided out of funds raised at a great bazaar. Under the guidance of Alexander Sturrock the school undertook pioneering systems of physical education which were to be reflected in education circles all over Scotland.

41.   The girls' class, Session 1909-10, High School, Dundee, during the Rectorship of John Maclennan, MA.

42. Pinafored, scrubbed and brushed, pupils pose with their teacher at Glamis school *circa* 1900. An infant school had been established at Glamis in 1834 and a school and schoolhouse was built in 1839. Two schoolmasters predominated in education at Victorian Glamis, Rev David Cowper (1773-1855) and Robert Grant Ross (d.1889).

43. A girls' class of the old Inverbrothock School, St Vigean's Road, Arbroath, *circa* 1900, with Miss Findlay (left) and Miss Stirling (right). The girls are all neatly dressed for this special school photograph set against a backdrop.

44. The 'half-timers' school' for Green's Mill and Baltic Works, Arbroath, 1887, the year of Queen Victoria's Diamond Jubilee. It was also the jubilee of the flax millowner, Andrew Lowson, who owned the school. The children worked half-time in the flax mills and went half-time to school. Green's Mill has long disappeared but the Baltic Works is now a whisky bond. One of Arbroath's most famous 'half-timers' was Sir Harry Lauder (1870-1950) who went to the school at Gordon's Mill. Although bright, the picture is a fine example of the rather bleak and functional buildings erected by the school boards in the three decades following the Education (Scotland) Act of 1872; although in this case Andrew Lowson had funded the school out of his own pocket. The children sit on hard wooden benches affixed to a common desk. On the wall are pictures of the British Empire, upon which the sun was deemed never to set. Much of the elementary school learning was of a dreary functional nature and repetitive in method. Education was funded in the public sector by a local levy and parents were expected to pay a school fee of around 2d to 3d (1-1.5p) per week; if they were unable to pay the fee they could apply to the parochial board for poor relief. In 1890 Lord Salisbury's Conservative government made more funds available so elementary education became virtually 'free'. The Education (Scotland) Act of 1908 gave school boards even wider powers and now they were required to make regular medical examinations and supervise children's welfare at school; legal action could now be taken against parents who allowed their children to go dirty, verminous or play truant.

CHAPTER SIX

CHILDHOOD MEMORIES

45. Lady Elizabeth Bowes Lyon, outside the main entrance to Glamis Castle, 1915. To be known in the 1920s and 1930s as 'the smiling Duchess', and the wartime Queen who refused to leave London during the blitz – and the most active and beloved dowager queen in British history – Lady Elizabeth spent much of her childhood years between the English and Scottish homes of the Strathmores; St Paul's, Walden Bury, Hertfordshire; Streatlam Castle, Co Durham; and Glamis Castle. She was also a frequent visitor to London where her father, the 14th Earl of Strathmore, owned 20 St James's Place.

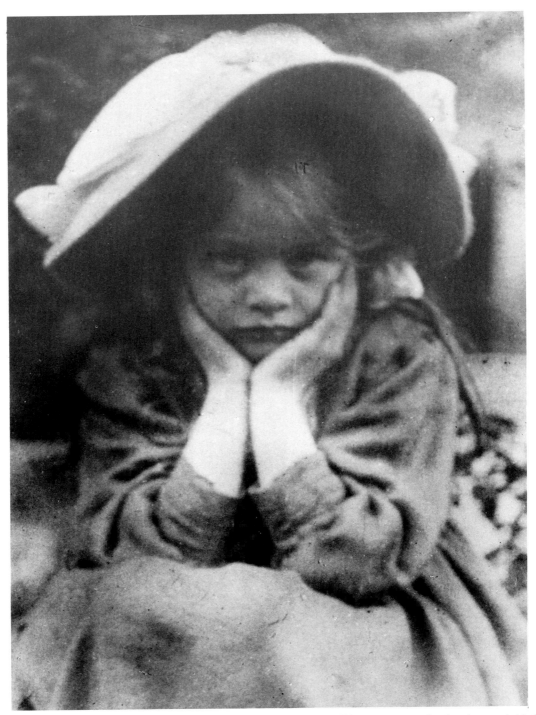

46. Tibbie Taggart of Brechin in her best bonnet pensively surveys David Waterson, watercolourist, the man behind the camera for this photograph of 1906. In later life Tibbie became a schoolteacher. Edwardian social historians described 1900 as the beginning of the 'childrens' century'. The first nursery school was opened in 1900; in 1902 the compulsory registration of midwives was achieved and in 1906 school meals started to be provided. Great steps indeed when it is remembered that it was only in 1867 that the Gangs Act prohibited the use of child labour for those under eight years of age.

47. A fisher family, Fountain Square, Auchmithie, 1890s. Many of the fisher-folk had nicknames and here we see 'Rab' mending nets, 'Nellie Bottlie' and 'Willie Father'. These were the days before state benefits for the poor. The foundation stone of the Welfare State did not come until Dec 1911 when the National Insurance Bill was passed.

48. Angus Folk Museum, in the sequestered Kirk Wynd of Glamis village, was developed from cottages presented to the National Trust for Scotland by the 16th Earl of Strathmore in 1957. This delightful children's group of the early 1900s shows the contemporary fashions in children's clothes. The museum contains many interesting items of period clothing.

49. Lady Elizabeth Bowes Lyon, with Juno, at Glamis Castle, 1911. She had acquired her courtesy title on 16 Feb 1904 on the death of her grandfather, the 13th Earl of Strathmore and Kinghorne. In 1908 she attended the school run by Constance Goff at 25 Marylebone High St, London, and in the same year made her first public appearance as bridesmaid at the wedding of her eldest brother, Patrick Bowes Lyon, Lord Glamis, to Lady Dorothy Osborne, the third daughter of the Duke of Leeds.

50. Mrs Margaret Paton of Montrose, nicknamed 'Buckie Meg' with her family. Mrs Paton and the children wear the fashions popular during 1895-1900; her cape has the fashionable raised collar; blouses developed during this decade from the short-like garment called the 'garibaldi' (after the Italian general). The boy seated on a cushion became Captain Robert Scott Paton.

51. Holidaymakers – more than likely from Dundee – pose against a backcloth of Broughty Ferry Castle, in the early 1900s. The photograph was probably taken either in the studio of Rodger or of Brown, at Broughty Ferry.

52. Labelled 'Lady Maclaren at Home' by an Edwardian wag, this print shows a tinker mother suckling her child. They are thought to be of the Maclaren family. Some tinkers camped in groups, others in family units. Usually tinkers considered themselves to be totally independent of marriage. Children were generally well-treated by their tinker parents; even so, schooling was considered valueless apart from its providing of the rudimentary writing skills.

53. This young Edwardian is a little doubtful about his being transported across the river South Esk by wire and in a 'game bag'. Like his peers, socially the boy's lifestyle was steadily improving with the new legislation of the Liberal Prime Ministers, Sir Henry Campbell-Bannerman and H H Asquith. Even so a boy born in the early years of the new century only had a life expectation of around 40 years while a girl might expect to live to be 42.

54. A telegram boy and barefooted urchin stand at the foot of St Andrew's St, Dundee, looking down the Seagate, the heart of Old Dundee, where the Tolbooth and Cross was once located. At the corner right is the office of Fairweather & Sons Ltd, Tobacco Manufacturers, 108 Seagate (now demolished). The Customs Warehouse and Trades Lane are off to the left. Telegram boys were usually the envy of their pals because of their distinctive uniforms and the bicycles they used. The earliest telegraphy took place in Great Britain in 1837 and the Post Office took over the telegram service in 1870.

CHAPTER SEVEN

WEDDINGS, VISITS, ACCIDENTS
AND ROYAL PROCLAMATIONS

55.   An Auchmithie wedding, *circa* 1895. Most weddings were solemnised some four miles away at St Vigeans church. The wedding party walked there preceded by Auchmithie's oldest woman who danced along carrying a glass of whisky. At the half-way point – the lodge gates of Seaton estate – the party would pause to partake of 'drams' and dance a reel or two.

56.   A 'scramble' at Auchmithie. Children would entreat all visitors to throw them halfpennies – particularly wedding parties. The latter was a survival of the old Scottish 'penny weddings' – when coin was the main marriage gift (or a 'lucky penny' handed to the bride) – the scramble often consisted of pennies and half-pennies heated on a coal shovel and pitched out of an open window to the local urchins.

57. George Claridge Druce unveils the memorial to George Don (1764-1814) at Forfar Parish Church (now the East and Old Parish Church) on 8 September 1910. George Don, the famous botanist, held the post of Principal Gardener of the Royal Botanical Gardens, Edinburgh, and established a Botanical Garden at Forfar.

58. The laying of the foundation stone of the present East Church, Barry. It was opened for public worship in Dec, 1888, and was built on the site of a previous church. A church is known to have existed here from the early eleventh century, under the patronage of the Cistercian abbey of St Edward at Balmerino, Fife.

59. Laying the foundation stone, Tulloch Hill Tower, 31 Aug 1901, by the 12th Earl of Airlie. The tower was built in memory of David, 11th Earl of Airlie, who was killed in the South African War on 11 June 1900 at the Battle of Diamond Hill. Lord Airlie had led the 12th Lancers during the rout of the Boers.

60. A smiling Countess of Airlie opens Dundee Flower Show, 29 August 1907, at Magdalen Green, Dundee. The platform party included the monocled Lord Provost William Longair; president of the Dundee Horticultural Society, Duncan Macdonald; and Ex-Lord Provost William Hunter. Behind are seen the bandsmen of the 2nd Battalion Highland Light Infantry under Bandsman C R Bicks.

61. General William Booth (1829-1912) of the Salvation Army at Friockheim, 9 September 1904. Born in Nottingham, Booth had become an itinerant Methodist preacher, but left the Methodists to conduct evangelistic work among the poor. He established a mission in Whitechapel, London, in 1865. The great reluctance of established churches to accept Booth's converts from the slums led to his foundation of the Salvation Army, with himself as General (1877). Friockheim (pronounced *Freek-um*) lies in the Parish of Kirkden, and General Booth is standing in an open-top automobile in Gardyne St at its junction with Millgate. To the left is Friockheim Church (united with Kinnell in 1967) which was disjoined from Kirkden in 1835. A church hall was erected next to the hotel in 1910. The church clock dates from 1885. Wilson's Railway Hotel is now the Railway Inn, and E. Suttie's cycle agency has now grown into Suttie's Garage at 1 Millgate.

62.　The snowstorms of 1906 caused havoc on the Angus railways. Here engine 708 of the Caledonian Railway, languishes at
　　　Rossie, near Montrose. The scene became a popular postcard of the period and the photographer was Milne of Brechin.

63.　Elliot Junction Rail Disaster, 28 Dec 1906. Some mile and a half southwest of Arbroath the LNER/LMS line joined with
　　　a line from the Carmyllie slate quarries; the gradients on this line were the highest in the world (except for Peru). At Elliot
　　　station a North British Railway 'special' out of Arbroath and bound for Edinburgh, collided with a stationary Caledonian
　　　Railway train. There were twenty-one fatalities.

64. Lord Provost William Longair reads a message of welcome to HM Queen Alexandra on the occasion of her embarking on the royal yacht *Victoria & Albert* on Monday, 24 August 1908, at Craig Pier, Dundee. The Queen was accompanied by her daughter, HRH the Princess Victoria, and was met at Dundee station by the civic party and Mabell, Countess of Airlie; the Hon Charlotte Knollys, the Queen's lady-in-waiting, Lady Abercrombie and Lady Helen Ogilvy, were also in attendance. The men in the forefront of the picture are baillies, civic dignitaries and gentlemen-in-waiting. The Queen, in a grey tweed costume and a feather boa, was about to embark on the pinnace that would take her to the royal yacht moored in the Tay with its escort ship *HMS Juno*. On the right, in the pinnace, is the royal yacht's commander, Rear-Adm Sir Colin Keppel. The Queen was on her way to Christiania (Oslo) to visit her Scandinavian relatives; she was the eldest daughter of HM King Christian IX of Denmark who had died two years earlier. In the background crowds have boarded the famous Tay vessel *Fifeshire* to obtain a better view.

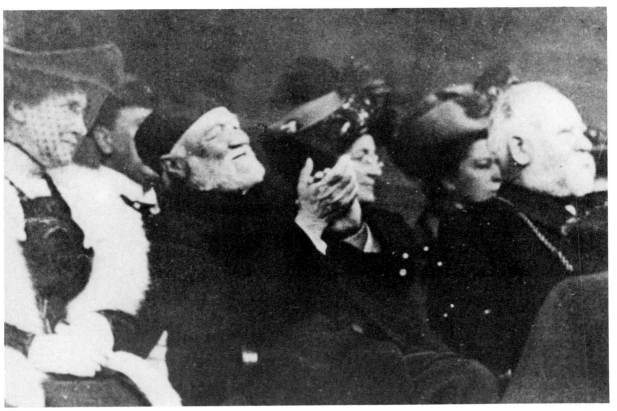

65.   Andrew Carnegie (1835-1919), manufacturer and philanthropist, applauds at the opening of Forfar Public Baths, 1910. In 1901 Carnegie had sold his profitable steel assets and retired in order to devote himself to distributing his wealth. His benefactions included endowments to libraries, civic amenities and 'hero funds' and the Carnegie Trust was to become wellknown in Angus from its support of such enterprises as parish halls and sports facilities. In 1908 Andrew Carnegie offered the sum of £6000 to provide public baths in Forfar. His offer was accepted by the Town Council, and plans went ahead to site the baths at the foot of the Vennel, on ground donated by Don Brothers Buist & Co Ltd. The architect of the project was H J Bland, Edinburgh. The baths were formally opened by Andrew Carnegie on Tuesday 4 October 1910; on that occasion Carnegie received the Freedom of the Burgh

66. The proclamation of King Edward VII outside the Town Hall (now the Courthouse), Arbroath, 25 June 1901. Queen Victoria had died on 19 June at Osborne House, Isle of Wight. The new king's coronation had to be postponed until 9 August 1902 because of his contraction of perityphlitis.

67. A drum-head service at Glamis Castle to present new colours to the Black Watch. The Royal Highland Regiment, the Black Watch, developed from the Independent Companies formed (1624) to 'watch' the Highlands. The 14th Earl of Strathmore and Kinghorne was Hon. Col of the 5th Angus and Dundee Battalion (1904) here represented.

CHAPTER EIGHT

RURAL FOLK

FOR centuries the land and the farms of Angus dominated the working population and affected the prosperity of the county. With the development of the railways the produce of Angus farms and small holdings found its way not only into the towns and villages of Eastern Scotland but far beyond. Angus was well known as an arable county, its cereals, root crops and grass being converted into fat cattle and sheep. Once even Irish store bred cattle were brought to Angus for fattening.

From around the 1850s to World War I, Angus agriculture depended principally on livestock production for economic survival. The year 1808, of course, had been a significant date in the history of Angus cattle rearing. In that year Hugh Watson of Keillor went to the Trinity Fair, Brechin, and purchased ten black heifers and a bull; to these were added six cows and a bull given to Watson by his father, and that made up the foundation herd of Aberdeen-Angus.

The breeding and rearing of cattle was mostly done on the slopes of the Sidlaws and in such glens as Glenisla, Glen Clova and Glenesk. Auction markets were established in the late Victorian years at Arbroath, Brechin and Montrose for the weekly sales of fat and store cattle, sheep and pigs. From such auctions were established the famous Aberdeen-Angus and Shorthorn pedigree bull sales.

During Victorian and Edwardian times the private landlord was the dominant figure and between 1870 and 1922 the best arable land in Angus was rented at around £3 per acre. The nineteenth century aristocrats, however, saw their responsibilities for the management of their lands eroded by the development of local government. They were relieved of the burden of road and bridge building and the promotion of education, and turned to gambling, race-horse breeding and hunting.

Since 1900, mechanisation has slowly driven the Angus agricultural workers from the land, but in these pages we see the old-time rural folk at work and at leisure. Once they were the backbone of the county and richly deserve pictorial immortality.

68. Sheep shearing at Ledmore, *circa* 1900. By the 1850s, sheep, mostly Blackface, had taken over the Angus hill farms. As time passed the ewes were crossed with Border Leicester tups to produce Greyfaced lambs; these were ultimately crossed with a Down breed of sheep.

69. David Lowden of Greenburn Croft with his daughter Nellie, *circa* 1910. Lowden cuts the crop with a shielded scythe. The water supply for the croft was obtained from across the bridge, top right. Attempts to regularise water supplies and drainage in Angus took place 1855-75.

70. Ploughmen with their horses, Edzell area, at the turn of the nineteenth century. This was the age of the horse. According to a government survey of 1884 there were more than two million horses on British farms alone, compared with 6000 one hundred years later.

71. Farmworkers and their families, Newbigging Farm, by Arbroath. Cheap imported food hit the very foundations of rural life in Angus, but the resilient farmers hit back with the production of high class seed and improved livestock from 1900 there was a greater use of fertilisers.

72. An Edwardian glen picnic at Glenqueich, near Cortachy. Note the barrel of Allsopp's ale and the watering can to catch the drips. The reveller on the extreme right is the gamekeeper turned policeman, Chay Smart, who was something of a local poet. The picture is by J L Tough of Kirriemuir.

73. The laird and the Glamis gamekeepers, a delightful conversation piece of *circa* 1890. *L. to R.*: The 13th Earl of Strathmore
    (with pipe); A Butchart; D Donaldson; W Fairweather; G Annand; W Crockett, two boys and a bowler-hatted groom.

74. A harvest scene in the Edzell area at the turn of the nineteenth century. Agriculture was labour intensive at this time, but
    by the end of World War I tractors were increasing sights in Angus. The lack of suitable tractor implements in the early
    days slowed down the mechanisation of the Angus farms. The advent of the pneumatic tyre in the 1920s and the improved
    implements for tractors sounded the knell both of the horse and the labourer.

75. Duncan Michie and wife, Jean Hay, two prominent 'Glenfolk' as pictured here from a print in the collection of the Glenesk Folk Museum. The museum contains a collection of nineteenth century wedding and kirkin' dresses, sunbonnets, mutches and shawls once favoured by the rural folk of the glen. The old couple are typical of the hardy folk who once peopled Scotland's glens.

76. Duncan Michie and the 'bothy boys' of Glenesk. Musical life in Angus around 1874 to 1910 was profuse and varied. Music was everywhere, in the home, in church, in the streets and developed in the schools as an integral part of education from the 1860s. Fiddle music was very popular, but the presence of a cello was rather rare in the far flung Victorian communities.

CHAPTER NINE

SPORTSMEN AND ELEPHANTS

AS Queen Victoria's reign gave way to that of her son, leisure time for the masses had grown enormously from the impetus engendered by the 1871 Bank Holiday Act, which had been introduced by Sir John Lubbock. The term 'recreation' had become a part of public service development and for the first time it was 'organised'.

Civic leaders had been eager to build on the provisions of the Libraries Act which had been extended to Scotland in 1854. The Act was further extended in 1892, and by 1894 H H Fowler's Local Government Act made it possible for every rural parish to have its free public library. Between 1886 and 1900 art galleries, museums, parks and gymnasia flourished, sponsored mostly out of local government and private funds and the masses were actively encouraged to use them.

Locally, associations such as the Glenisla Benevolent Society (1859) sponsored neighbourhood activites and latterly the Glenisla Highland Games. Rugby, curling, football and golf were all popular during this period, and the pictures show the sporting and leisure fads, fancies and fanaticism on offer to the Angus folk.

77.

Corinthians Football Club, 1908-09. Forfar

L to R.:
Back Row: V.T. McKenzie, Director; S. Kay; J. Henderson; W.L.M. Easton; J.W. Stewart, Hon Sec. and Treasurer.
Middle Row: Alf Peacock, Manager; A.F.B. Brown; W.S. Law; R.N. Balfour, Captain; J.S. Massie; J.C. Smart, Trainer.
Front Row: C. Edwards, President; W.R. McLaren; J.K. Duncan, Vice-Captain; D.H. Gourlay; R. Glen, Hon. Pres.
Seated; H.Stewart; L.K. Cuthbert.

Football as it is played today did not take shape until 1863, when the Football Association was established. The Scottish Football Association was founded in 1873, and the UK Football League was founded in 1888. Forfar Athletic F.C. was established in 1884. The F.A. Amateur Cup was instituted in 1892.

78. An elephant walks the tightrope at Forfar Games, Steele Park, *circa* 1910. Games and fairs continued to bring colour, novelty and excitement into the drab lives of the Angus proletariat. Forfar has two parks of historical interest. Reid Park was the gift of Provost Peter Reid (1803-97), a typical Victorian benefactor, and was opened in 1896 by John Morley MP for Angus Burghs. Steele Park is the recreation ground adjoining Reid Park and was presented to the burgh by David Steele of Beech Hill.

79. Dalhousie Golf Club House, Links Parade, Carnoustie, *circa* 1905, from the photograph by Valentine & Sons. The Club was formed in 1868 by a group of Dundee businessmen. It was named after the Rt Hon Fox Maule, Earl of Dalhousie, its first patron. The Club was one of the 24 clubs which were responsible for the foundation of the British Amateur Championship, 1886.

80. Sold as a postcard with the caption 'The Latest Craze, American Roller Skating, Dundee', this picture is pre-1909. It was the invention of ball-bearings which facilitated roller-skating, and the craze, called 'Rinkomania', was rife in the 1870s and again in the early 1900s.

81. The circus winds its way along Montrose St, Cadger Hillock, Brechin, *circa* 1900. This picture comes from a lantern slide and shows houses on the Gas Works side of the street, Den Burn Works and Union St. The cathedral is seen faintly through the haze at the far end of the street.

82. Airlie football team, taken in the garden of Cortachy Castle, *circa* 1902. Second from the right, front row, is the Rt. Hon. David, 12th Earl of Airlie, then aged about nine; he had succeeded to the title when he was seven when his father, the 11th Earl, was killed during the South African War.

83. Brechin Cricket XI playing a visitors' match at Glamis Castle. The *mid row* shows the Brechin team stalwarts Freeman, Hollingsworth, O'Neil, Ferrier and Smith (who was a professional). The Brechin Cricket Club had been established in 1849. The team were the guests of the 14th Earl of Strathmore and Kinghorne himself an accomplished fast bowler.

84. The 13th Earl of Strathmore and Kinghorne entertains his guests at a picnic lunch on his grouse moor during one of the season's shoots. The Earl is seated on the far right of the back row in the box; his keepers and beaters stand to the left of the box. Note the picnic hampers.

85. The organ grinder and his monkey entertain the appreciative crowd at the Cross, Carnoustie, *circa* 1900. Street entertainment had been popular from medieval times; exotic animals, from bears to elephants, always drew the crowds in the largely unsophisticated society of rural Angus. Another favourite crowd-puller in Victorian times were the 'blackamoors', coloured musicians and tumblers from circuses.

CHAPTER TEN

HARBOURS, SHIPS AND FISHERFOLK

86. Dundee harbour and docks, *circa* 1896. The original prosperity of Dundee was based on its status as a Royal Burgh, its market, its ferry traffic with Fife and its sea-trade. By the early seventeenth century it had a prosperous linen trade with Norway and England, an import trade with Sweden and commerce with Danzig, Koenigsberg and Riga. The Scottish engineer, Thomas Telford (1757-1834), produced an extensive floating dock and graving dock for large vessels, completed in 1826. The picture shows the King William IV Dock which had been completed in 1834. The site was cleared to accommodate the approach roads for the modern Tay Road Bridge. The expansion of Dundee's dockland was linked with the Jute trade from India and the North Atlantic whaling fleet. By 1912 Dundee harbour occupied 190 acres. To the left of the picture lay the Greenmarket, at the foot of Crichton St. The spire of St Paul's Episcopal Cathedral (1853) at Castle Hill, rises above the Exchange Coffee House (1828 – now Winter's, Shore Terrace).

87. Lantern slide of Arbroath harbour with herring being packed into barrels by pipe-smoking fisher-women, *circa* 1880. Most of the barrels were made on site. During the herring season Arbroath's harbour bustled but herring was last landed in any quantity in 1953.

88. The Australian liner *Ulimaroa* runs ashore opposite James Place, Foreshore, West Ferry, on Monday, 2 December 1907. While on her trial trip the 5700-ton *Ulimaroa* came to grief because of a 'derangement in the steering gear' noted contemporary commentators. The vessel had been built by Gourlay Brothers & Co Ltd for Huddart, Parker & Co, Melbourne, Australia, at the Camperdown Shipyard. *Ulimaroa* had been launched on 11 July 1907 and was destined for the inter-colonial passenger and cargo trade. She was pulled off the West Ferry foreshore by the Tay tugs *Gilroy* and *Renown* on Tuesday, 3 December 1907.

89. Fisher-children gather by the shore at Ferryden, 13 June 1896. Ferryden, at the mouth of the South Esk, three-quarters of a mile south of Montrose, was once a fishing village of note. Montrose men were regularly stoned out of the village in case they courted the local girls, thus decimating the very low-waged female labour force.

90. Montrose fishing boats, 13 June 1896. Between 1840-88 Montrose harbour had its heyday, busy with cargoes of salmon, grain, potatoes and timber. Indeed during the period 1860-80, Montrose ranked second in Scotland to Greenock as a timber importing port. The vessels display the registration letters ME for Montrose.

91. 'Salmon-fishing' on the South Esk at Montrose', reads the caption of this old photograph. The burgh's port had long acted as a maritime centre for the rich agricultural hinterland. Here Scandinavian wood and iron were imported and grain and salmon exported. In 1837 the harbour was bought from the Town Council by a body of landowners and burghers.

92. The entrance to the tidal harbour, Arbroath, *circa* 1890; note the brigantine on the left as it enters the harbour. This slow, rather cumbersome, type of sailing vessel had two masts, square-rigged on the foremast, with a fore-and-aft mainsail and square topsails. They had few facilities for passengers who had to take second place to the cargo.

CHAPTER ELEVEN

CORTACHY CASTLE AND THE OGILVY FAMILY

SET at a bend of the River South Esk, the much-altered Cortachy Castle, stems from a court-yard style castle of the 15th century. Although tradition has it that Cortachy was a hunting-lodge used by King Robert I, the Bruce, the castle today is set on the site of a 14th century castle, then belonging to the Stewart Earls of Strathearn.

Cortachy was granted by a charter of King James II to Sir Walter Ogilvy of Oures in 1473. In time his kinsman, Thomas Ogilvy of Clova, acquired the castle, Then in 1625 it was sold by Sir David Ogilvy to James, first Earl of Airlie.

Charles II is said to have stayed at Cortachy on 7 October 1650. Tired of being lectured by the prating Lords of the Congregation while at Perth, the story goes, Charles slipped away on the pretext of going hawking. He joined his friend Lord Airlie at Cortachy. Still today, the chamber in which he slept is called 'the King's Room'. The Covenanters came in search of him, but he fled through a secret tunnel to Glen Clova; he was discovered in a small cottage. In 1651 Cortachy was sacked by the troops of Oliver Cromwell under General George Monck. When the Airlie estate was set to the torch again by the Covenanting Earl of Argyll in 1691, the Ogilvys made Cortachy their main home.

Strong Jacobites, the Ogilvys supported Charles Edward Stuart in his attempt to secure the throne for his father Prince Francis Edward, the 'Old Pretender'. After the defeat of the Jacobites at Culloden by HRH William Augustus, Duke of Cumberland, in 1746, David, Lord Ogilvy fled to France his titles attained. There he sat out a 32 year exile but rose to be a lieutenant-general in Louis XV's army and commanded Ogilvy's Regiment. The lands and titles were not restored until 1826.

The 10th Earl of Airlie (1826-81), was responsible for much enlargement and alteration at Cortachy, which was continued by the 11th Earl (1856-1900) who employed the well-known architect David Bryce, famous for his 'Scottish Baronial' style.

93. Victorian Cortachy showing the alterations made by the 10th and 11th Earls of Airlie. A great deal of the Scottish baronial wings was demolished by the 12th Earl.

94.	The Ogilvy heirs pose at Cortachy:
L. to R.; The Hon Bruce Arthur Ashley Ogilvy (1895-1973). An officer in the 12th Lancers, he served as Equerry to the Prince of Wales. The Hon Patrick Julian Harry Stanley Ogilvy (b.1896. A captain in the Irish Guards, he was killed in action in 1917). Lord Ogilvy (1893-1968). An officer in the 10th Hussars, he served in World War I. He succeeded his father as the 12th Earl of Airlie in 1900. Lord Chamberlain to Her Majesty Queen Elizabeth the Queen Mother.

CHAPTER TWELVE

THE ANGUS FOLK AT HOME

95. Children pose for the camera at the Barrack Park, Dudhope Castle, 22 May 1896. Dudhope Castle, built at the close of the sixteenth century, was the fortress home of the Constable of Dundee. The last owner to live in the castle was Lord Douglas of Douglas; his successor, the Victorian 12th Earl of Home, was the 27th and last Titular Constable. Following the French Revolution a 'sympathy riot' took place in Dundee in 1792. Thereafter the government sub-leased Dudhope Castle as a military headquarters. It remained a barracks until August 1880. The castle and grounds were bought by the city in 1893. The policies of the castle were long used as military parade grounds, and troops were stationed here during the two world wars.

96. A family pose conveniently in their carriage in Whitehall Crescent, Dundee, 9 July 1897, to set off the shop fronts. Whitehall Crescent had been 'improved' by architect, Robert Keith, and others during 1885-9. The 'school' in the centre of the picture was exploiting the inventions of Sir Isaac Pitman and John Robert Gregg; and the typewriter invented in 1868 by Scholes, Gliden and Soule.

97. The High St, Dundee, in the late years of Victoria's reign. Here markets were once held, and the cab is from the rank which always stood east of the Town House, which is off to the right. By the 1890s, Smith Brothers (the site of the Royal Bank, 1899) had opened their large drapery emporium at No 4, next to Tyndal's Wynd. St Paul's Episcopal Cathedral rises above the Royal British Hotel at Castle Hill.

98. The High St, Dundee, 5 July 1895. Fleming & Haxton, shipping agents, were still at No 44 High St, for this picture was taken a few years before their move to No 76. Strathtay House, on the corner of Reform St (1832) and the Old Overgate, were the premises of Adam Smail 'boys', and youths' clothier, girls' costumier and gentlemen's outfitter' from the early 1870s. After the death of Adam Smail, it was run under the same name by trustees up to World War I, when it was taken over by the Manfield Boot and Shoe Co, and is today Boots the Chemists.

99. A scene in the Vault, Dundee 27 May 1904. Rising above is the Town House built by William Adam in 1732, one of Dundee's most gracious Georgian buildings. It stood on the south side of the High Street on the site of today's City Square.

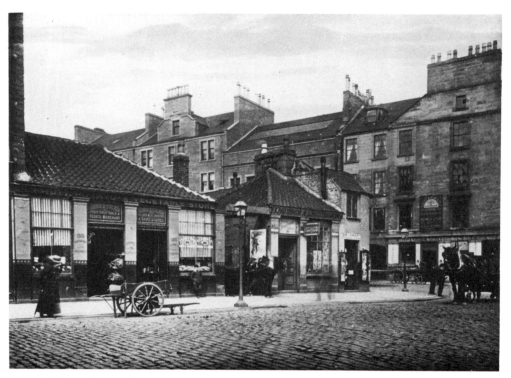

100. Dock St, Dundee, at the turn of the century. On the right is the headquarters of the Dundee & Newcastle Steam Shipping Co Ltd whose 'flagship' was the *SS Alderney*.

101. Steam-driven roundabouts at Dundee's Greenmarket. The Greenmarket was situated at the foot of Crichton St, and the junction of Shore Terrace. Markets were held here chiefly on Fridays and Saturdays. The stalls boasted sweets, flowers, fish, meat, all kinds of foods, among which stood fiddlers, pickpockets, organ grinders, whores, auctioneers and street preachers.

102. Loungers stand and shopkeepers gaze in this Edwardian view of the junction of Dock Street and Commercial St, Dundee. Note the gable end with the wide range of advertising. Advertising developed as the multiple stores like Liptons and the Maypole vied with each other to promote a faster turnover. As befits a maritime city the Navigation School is seen left.

103. The Weigh House and Salt Store at Whitehall Crescent, Dundee, photographed from Dock St. The 'Tall Turret' in the centre of the picture is a part of Gilfillan Memorial Church, designed by Malcolm Stark in 1887. The church was named after Rev George Gilfillan (1813-78), the celebrated social reformer.

104. Erskine United Free Church, formerly the United Presbyterian Church, Dundee St, Carnoustie. It was later converted into the Regal Cinema. Today part of the site is used by the Royal British Legion. Construction work is seen to the right on the present Carnoustie Church. Designed by Robert Baldie, Glasgow, Erskine UF Church was opened in 1873 by the Earl of Dalhousie.

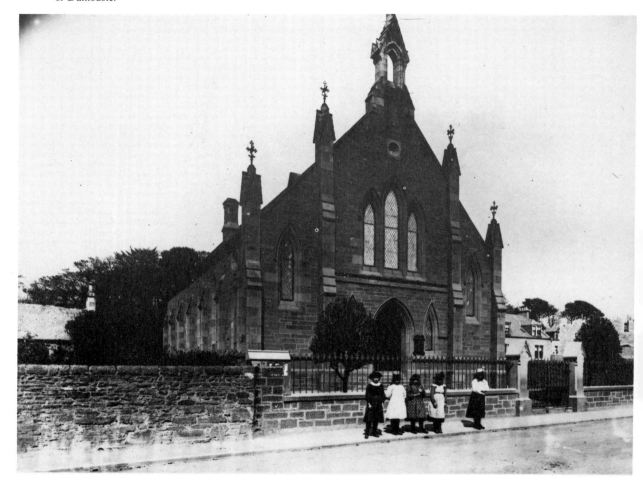

105. Carnoustie Municipal Buildings, High St. The premises with the window blind on the right are now the Tourist Information Office. In its early days the Town Council met in a small shop in the High St until the Municipal Buildings were established in 1896, considered by many a 'riotous extravagance'. The print is by Dugald Colquhoun and was published by Alexander Buik, Printer, Stationer and House Agent in his publicity booklet.

106. A now vanished scene at the coastal village of East Haven, 1870, in the parish of Panbride. Once the community won a hard living from the sea; lobsters went to London; crabs for the tables of Angus; haddock for Dundee and Forfar; and during the winter the boats used cod-lines. The fish was usually salted and exported.

107. A Valentine & Co photograph of the Old Manse and Church, Liff. The gothic parish church was constructed in 1839 to replace one built in 1774; but, Liff was mentioned in connection with the Augustinian priory of Scone in 1107. The imposing spire was the work of William Mackenzie.

108. A good bag of rabbits for the two shooters outside Mrs Reid's Post Office at Lethnot, in the parish of Lethnot, northwest of Brechin. In 1800 the parish sported six tailors, seven weavers, two smiths and two wrights, but around the time the photograph was taken, *circa* 1900, the population had shrunk by half.

109. A Valentine & Co picture of the Mansion House, Auchterhouse, a sixteenth century building, the erstwhile home of the Ramsays, Stewarts, Buchans, Lyons and Ogilvys and latterly the home of William H Valentine of Spalding & Valentine Ltd, jute and rayon manufacturers. Today it is the tastefully converted Old Mansion House Hotel.

110. Greystane House, Invergowrie, the home of the 'Home Rule progressive Liberal' David M. Watson (1835-1901), *circa* 1870, looking towards Liff. The tall baronial tower house, with fine plaster and timberwork, was built for David Watson by Campbell Douglas. Watson had taken over the Bullionfield Paper Works at Invergowrie in 1861, from the Cowan family. The paper mill had been started in Invergowrie by Charles Cowan in 1850; Charles Heron Watson, David's son, sold the paper mill in 1919 and it closed in 1965. On his death David Watson was survived by eleven children, and the family moved from the house after one of David Watson's daughters died in a tragic accident. The house remained the residence of the changing owners of the paper mill, the last of whom, Andrew A K Wright, lived there from 1931 until 1965 when it was bought by two local businessmen to run as a private hotel; one of the partners married the actress Jill Gascoine. The hotel was later sold to Ushers Brewery who subsequently were taken over by Lorimers Brewers soon to merge with Vaux Breweries. Greystane House joined the Swallow hotels group in 1977 and an annex was built on to the old building in 1979, on the site of the former gardens in the photograph's foreground. The old gates (now vanished) to Greystane House once belonged to the enclosure around St Paul's cathedral, London. The united parish of Invergowrie (with Liff and Benvie) was placed by the Boundary Commissioners in Forfarshire in 1891 and the name Invergowrie (formerly Mylnefield Feus) was generally accepted by 1912. The house is now surrounded on its south side by the Kingsway West by-pass from Dundee/Perth.

111. Brechin Mechanics, Literary and Scientific Institution (1835), at the junction of St Mary's and Church St, 1 June 1889. In the lower floor of the Institute was housed the Grammar school, and the parish and burgh schools. A separate High School was built and opened in 1877. The Institute was funded by Baron Panmure of Brechin and Novar (1771-1852). In front of the Institute is seen the memorial fountain of 1877 to Fox Maule Ramsay, 11th Earl of Dalhousie and Baron Panmure; the fountain was moved to St Ninian Square in 1894.

112. The Muckle market, High St, Brechin. These markets were formerly held on the first Tuesday after 28th May and 28th November, wherein took place the 'feeing' of farm servants. In Victorian and Edwardian times Brechin market was held over three days, preceded by a horse parade and sale, held in Clerk St. This market around the Cross comprises stalls selling cheap goods.

113. Women knitting by the roadside in Edzell High Street, *circa* 1880. The area is now built over and the roadway developed, but here we see it as a Victorian hamlet. The proprietors of the parish were the Earls of Dalhousie, and the handsome archway through which the village is now entered, the 'Dalhousie Archway', was erected in 1887 as a memorial to the 13th Earl of Dalhousie and his Countess.

114. The Royal Jubilee Arms Hotel, Dykehead, in the parish of Cortachy and Clova, 19 August 1893. The scene shows how popular this area was with Victorian and Edwardian trippers from the industrial south and west. It was a region much loved by Captain Robert Falcon Scott and Dr Edward Adrian Wilson who reached the South Pole in 1912 and who died together on the Great Ice Barrier in the same year.

115. Joseph Hume's statue dominates the junction of High St and Hume St, Montrose in this picture taken on 11 April 1892. Joseph Hume (1777-1855), was brought up by a widowed mother who used to sell crockery in Montrose market. He made his fortune in the East India Company and became a radical politician. He sat as Liberal MP for Montrose District of Burghs and advocated free trade; he opposed flogging in the army and consistently questioned governmental expenditure. The statue was erected in 1859, and is the work of Calder Marshall, ARA. When excavations were being made for the siting of the statue a silver hoard of Edward I's reign was discovered; a cache no doubt secreted when there were houses down the middle of the High St.

116. Montrose Basin and old suspension bridge, 13 June 1896. Founded by the charter of King David I, Montrose is set on the east of the tidal basin formed by the estuary of the river South Esk. The basin is navigable at high tide, and is the gathering ground of winter geese. The old suspension bridge was erected in 1828 and demolished to make way for a new concrete bridge in 1928.

117. St Thomas Tavern, by the West Gate, Arbroath Abbey, 1880s. The inn took its name from the dedicatee of the Benedictine abbey next door. St Thomas Becket of Canterbury, archbishop and martyr (1179). Set at Tower Neuk, the tavern was replaced in the 1890s and the site cleared in the 1930s to make way for a garden.

118. George W Donald (b. 1820), custodian of Arbroath Abbey, stands in the nave of his famous charge. A celebrated local poet, one of his duties was to stand at the gate, for the entry of funerals into the Abbey Burial Ground. The abbey was founded for the grey-robed Benedictine monks from the French order at Tiron in 1178 by King William the Lion. After the Reformation the abbey fell into decay and clearance and renovations were made in the 1830s and 1890s. The Abbot's House was acquired in 1905 by the Office of Works and was opened as a museum in 1934.

119. The Croft Market, East High St, Forfar, 1870. The Croft markets were held every Wednesday and, according to the antiquarian and educationalist, Alan Reid, in his *The Royal Burgh of Forfar* (1902), were 'the survivals of the ancient fairs named in honour of St Margaret, St Etherman' and other of the guild saints. Along with the Michaelmas and Martinmas Term markets, the Croft Market was an important 'feeing' time for farm servants. The church in the top centre of the photograph is the Old Parish Church (now the East and Old), the successor of the church of Forfar founded in 1241 by David de Bernham, Bishop of St Andrews, and dedicated to St James the Great. The steeple dates from 1814-15.

120. The Square, Kirriemuir, *circa* 1890, showing the strikingly odd Town House, the oldest building in the burgh, dating from 1604. Towering above the Drapery Warehouse (now the site of David Sim's Ironmonger) is the Old Parish Church, the work of David Playfair (1787); the steeple was a gift of Charles Lyell of Kinnordy, 1790. The clock was added in 1862. Edwards's emporium is long demolished.

121. The High St, Kirriemuir, 14 October 1895. Kirriemuir developed as a 'burgh of barony' in 1459 under the Douglas Earls of Angus. The East Angus Co-op Society now takes in the Victorian premises of William Philip, 18 High St, and Albion House. Today the Union Hotel, Bank St adjoins the building on the right. The Ogilvy Arms Hotel evolved from the Crown Hotel.

122. The roundabouts on East High St, Forfar *circa* 1900. Market and fair amusements were revolutionised in the 1860s through the application of steam power and again in the 1880s with the introduction of electricity.

123. A view down Castle St, Forfar *circa* 1890, before the construction of Irons, the ironmongers emporium, to the right.

124. 'Edzell for Holidays' proclaimed the old guide books, and the Glenesk Hotel, High St, Edzell was one of the most prominent in the area, seen here on 25 May 1898.

125. Edzell Castle, 25 May 1898, lies one mile west of the Victorian hamlet seen above, and this picture was taken before the refurbishment of the pleasance (walled garden). The seat of the Lindsay family, the Earls of Crawford, the 16th century castle replaced an earlier one set further north.

CHAPTER THIRTEEN

WORK FOR THE PEOPLE

126. Auchmithie fisherwomen, *circa* 1904. Women played a very large part in the fishing communities. Usually they were employed cutting, cleaning and smoking the fish caught, and baiting, or 'reddin' the lines. Their task too was to sell the fish in Dundee and Forfar and some of the carrying baskets are seen in this picture. It was a hard life and their status in society was low; indeed in 1705 the Earl of Northesk complained to the Town Council of Arbroath for luring the Auchmithie fisherfolk into the town. He maintained that the Authmithie fisherfolk were his serfs and were not free to move around as they pleased – his Lordship won his case. The nineteenth century was an age in which prices were as cheap as life. Government reports dated 1884, for instance, show that income tax was just one shilling (5p) in the pound. And beef was a tasty 5d (2p) a pound; eggs were 8½d (3½p) a dozen, and butter was just 10¼d (4.3p). Today's Angus inhabitant would need more than £32 to buy what his ancestor in 1884 could have bought for a pound sterling. Poor people in the nineteenth century were more likely to be destitute than in debt. The poor had to pay in cash and were not allowed the luxury of bills. Non-payment of rent led to swift eviction.

127. David Small & Sons, Seedsmen, Brechin. Employees at work in the loft of the seedsmen's shop filling sacks, weighing seed and preparing for delivery, *circa* 1910. The firm was established in 1896 when David Small bought an existing seedsman's business from James Young at 20 Swan St, Brechin. The firm closed down when the son of the founder retired in 1976.

128. The 'Back Shift' leaving Baxter Bros', Dens Works, *circa* 1908. Baxter Bros & Co Ltd, Linen & Jute Spinners and Manufacturers, were founded by William Baxter of Balgavies, who erected a flax spinning mill at Glamis in 1802. In 1822, in partnership with his eldest son, Edward, he built his first mill on the Dens Road, Dundee. During 1830, two other sons were assumed as partners and the firm was changed from William Baxter and Son to Baxter Bros & Co. It was incorporated as a limited company in 1892. The firm became a member of the Low & Bonar Group in 1924 and ceased trading in 1974.

129. The Royal Scots Greys, 2nd Dragoons, outside the Chance Inn, Inverkeilllor. Their parade was a part of a recruiting drive. The regiment had been founded in 1678 and took its name from its stone-grey uniforms; in 1687 the regiment was dressed in red coats lined with blue. The regiment served with honour at Waterloo (1815), the Crimean War (1854-56) and the South African War (1899-1902).

130. A shooting party pause for refreshment in the hills of Glenesk. Shooting was a very popular sport and brought the aristocracy and the gentry together to co-operate in common policies of game preservation. It was not uncommon for an Angus laird to hire a whole train to transport his guests, carriages, horses, dogs and beaters to the grouse moors from his English home.

131. A delightful 'conversation piece' of *circa* 1904 showing Auchmithie fisherwomen in their everyday costume. Fisherwomen usually wore a white 'mutch', a kirtled 'coat' and a canvas apron and sucked on a clay pipe called a 'cutty'. Footwear was the traditional wheeling stockings and heel-less 'bachles'.

(Overleaf)

132. A view of Barry Camp which was acquired by the government in the late years of Victoria's reign as a summer camp for troop training and military exercises.

133. Fisherwomen washing the family clothes at Arbroath. The picture is *circa* 1903 and formed a popular postcard in the W.R & S 'Reliable Series'.

134. Arbroath Railway Station Staff – and dog –*circa* 1900. The old station at Arbroath was replaced in 1911.

135. Carts fully laden outside the premises of David Small & Sons, Brechin, *circa* 1910. It was estimated that at the turn of the century one horse was needed for every 10 people to keep society going.

136. Dundee Flour Mills, Wheat Silos and Flour Warehouses, 4 May, 1909. The picture, which was sold in postcard form, shows the carters working for John F. White Ltd. The firm had been founded by Dr John F White (1830-1904) of Craigtay. It also shows the dependance on horse transport. There had been a good deal of ill-treatment of horses in Victorian and Edwardian times promoting the foundation of the RSPCA and the publication of Anna Sewell's novel 'Black Beauty' in 1877.

137. Combe, Barbour and Combe Ltd's machines at the Spinning Mill at Spring Gardens, Arbroath. The firm belonged to D & W Corsar, flax manufacturers.

138. Divers prepare to descend during the reconstruction of the dock gates at Arbroath in 1881.

139. A policeman strolls across the walkway of the old Dock Gates, Arbroath Harbour, 1888. *From L. to R.*, were located the Old Customs House, the Harbour Master's Office, and Ladybridge House. A popular location for the local urchins to fish for 'podlies'.

140. A delightful picture from The Signal Tower Museum, Arbroath, captioned 'Filling Pirns'. A 'pirn' is an old Scots word for
a small spool for holding the weft-yarn in the shuttle; a bobbin. The museum displays several spinning wheels. Before
Arbroath's flax industry became mechanised, the weaving of flax was carried out in the homes of weavers as a cottage
industry. The yarn supplied by several women was needed by just one weaver to produce a length of canvas on his loom.

141. The Staff of Carnoustie Public School, *circa* 1901. Mr Nicholson, Headmaster from 1875 to 1903, is pictured in the centre. During his time the school leaving age was still 10 and the amount spent on education in the United Kingdom, say in 1884, was £5.75 million (cf. £13.75 billion in 1984).

142. The night shift at J & D Wilkie's, Kirriemuir, *circa* 1887. The Kirriemuir Linen Works was founded in 1869 by brothers, John and David Wilkie; a weaving factory in which Sir James Barrie's father held a clerical post in the 1870's. The boy with the oil-can is George Cruickshanks, who had been born in 1872; members of his family still live in Kirriemuir, and J & D Wilkie's is still in business manufacturing jute and polypropylene goods.

143. Montrose fisherwomen pack herring in this lantern slide from a Victorian collection. Herring were gutted, salted and packed
by the women for export – much going to the Baltic. the sorting out of the herring was very important – *matties* were the
young fish; *fulls* the mature fish (with eggs or roe); and *spent* were the spawned fish. The herring were packed into barrels,
then examined by the Fishing Officer who branded each barrel and stencilled it with a crown mark.

144. A group of employees from D. J. Macdonald Ltd, Engineers and Machine Makers, South Saint Roque's Works, Dundee, *circa* 1900. They pose in front of one of the firm's overhead, hand-stitch, sack-sewing machines. Founded in 1892 by D J Macdonald (b. 1857), the company manufactured a wide range of machinery, but tended to specialise in those which were concerned with the finishing processes of textiles; sewing machines; printing machines; and proofing/impregnating machines. The company was voluntarily wound up in 1984 (though part was bought by Perth Foundry Ltd).

145. Arbroath Fire Brigade, *circa* 1903. The first fire brigade in the United Kingdom was organised in 1680, and a fire engine was patented in 1700. In 1829 the first steam fire engine was invented by Braithwaite. Motor fire engines were introduced in 1905.

146. Arbroath's new Steam Fire Engine, 1900. In the early days it was the Insurance Companies who provided fire fighting services. By 1749 there were hand-operated machines in Perth and a city fire brigade was established in 1835. In those days the Perth-based firemen assisted at fires in West Forfarshire. By 1809 Dundee had its own fire engine at School Wynd. The Angus Area Fire Brigade came into existence on 16 May 1948 when the Fire Service was transferred from the National Fire Service (1940) to Local Authority Councils. The new Tayside Fire Brigade was established on 16 May 1975.

147. The bar of the Crown Inn, Arbroath, 1890s. Photographs of the interiors of public houses and hotels are quite rare for this period. The well-polished and decorated fixtures of this bar show what a powerful attraction it must have been to those who lived in cramped, ill-lit housing. The publican of the local pub was generally an important figure in working-class society.

148. A handloom weaver, Kirriemuir, in the 1890s. When the power looms were introduced the traditonal looms died out, and in the 1900s they were more or less extinct. The bunches of threads above the loom were known as 'thrums', a term later used by Sir James Barrie for his fictionalised Kirriemuir.